TREASURES
OF THE
VATICAN
COLLECTIONS

TREASURES
OF THE

Alan Levy
ARTnews Foreign Correspondent

An Artpress Book

VATICAN
COLLECTIONS

A PLUME BOOK
NEW AMERICAN LIBRARY
TIMES MIRROR
NEW YORK AND SCARBOROUGH, ONTARIO

The publisher wishes to acknowledge the assistance generously provided by the curatorial staff of the Vatican Museums.

Artpress Books is the imprint of
Annellen Publications, Inc.
122 East 42nd Street
New York, New York 10017

PLUME TRADEMARK REG. U.S. PAT. OFF. AND FOREIGN COUNTRIES
REGISTERED TRADEMARK—MARCA REGISTRADA

SIGNET, SIGNET CLASSICS, MENTOR, PLUME, MERIDIAN and NAL BOOKS are published *in the United States* by The New American Library, Inc., 1633 Broadway, New York, New York, 10019, *in Canada* by The New American Library of Canada Limited, 81 Mack Avenue, Scarborough, Ontario MIL 1M8

First Plume Printing, February, 1983
1 2 3 4 5 6 7 8 9

Composition by Dix Type Co., Syracuse, New York
Printed and bound by Mandarin Offset International, Ltd., Hong Kong

ISBN 0-452-25393-4

CONTENTS

LIST OF ILLUSTRATIONS

*Indicates works scheduled at time of printing for inclusion in U.S. exhibition.

FLOOR PLAN OF THE VATICAN MUSEUMS

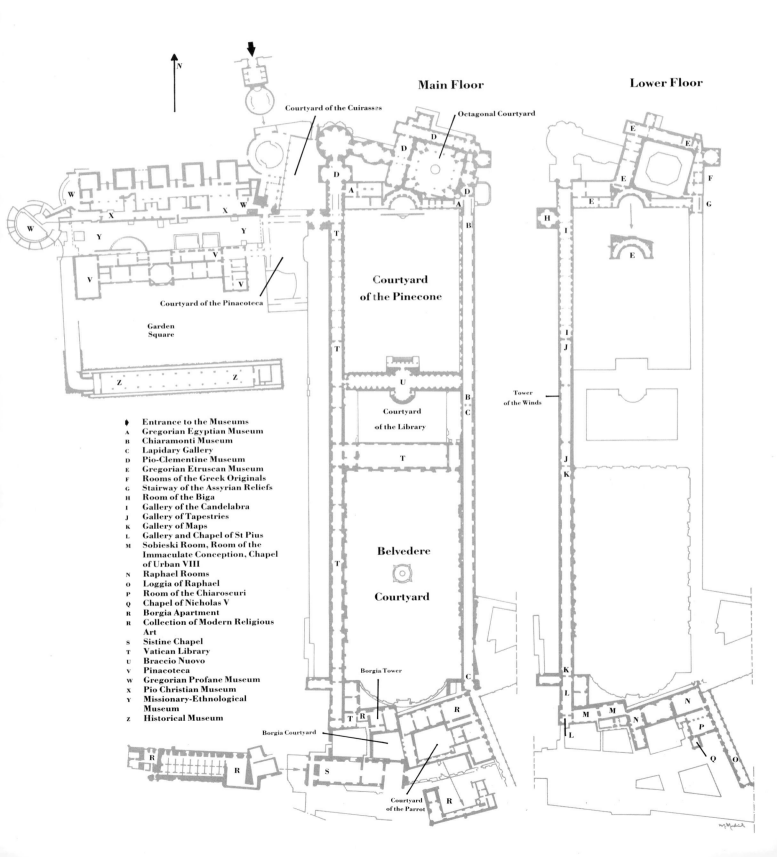

Main Floor

Lower Floor

Courtyard of the Cuirasses

Octagonal Courtyard

Courtyard
of the Pinecone

Courtyard of the Pinacoteca

Garden
Square

Courtyard
of the Library

Belvedere

Courtyard

Tower
of the Winds

Borgia Tower

Borgia Courtyard

Courtyard
of the Parrot

♦   **Entrance to the Museums**
A   **Gregorian Egyptian Museum**
B   **Chiaramonti Museum**
C   **Lapidary Gallery**
D   **Pio-Clementine Museum**
E   **Gregorian Etruscan Museum**
F   **Rooms of the Greek Originals**
G   **Stairway of the Assyrian Reliefs**
H   **Room of the Biga**
I   **Gallery of the Candelabra**
J   **Gallery of Tapestries**
K   **Gallery of Maps**
L   **Gallery and Chapel of St Pius**
M   **Sobieski Room, Room of the
    Immaculate Conception, Chapel
    of Urban VIII**
N   **Raphael Rooms**
O   **Loggia of Raphael**
P   **Room of the Chiaroscuri**
Q   **Chapel of Nicholas V**
R   **Borgia Apartment**
R   **Collection of Modern Religious
    Art**
S   **Sistine Chapel**
T   **Vatican Library**
U   **Braccio Nuovo**
V   **Pinacoteca**
W   **Gregorian Profane Museum**
X   **Pio Christian Museum**
Y   **Missionary-Ethnological
    Museum**
Z   **Historical Museum**

FOREWORD

OURISTS WHO VISIT THE VATICAN for the first time are often amazed to discover that the Holy See's art treasures are vast and wide-ranging—from Egyptian and Etruscan antiquities to a collection of modern art. The Vatican's art treasures are seldom allowed to travel, but many of them will come to the United States for the first time in 1983, when the Metropolitan Museum of Art in New York presents a special exhibition of art from the Holy See. These works will also be seen at the Art Institute of Chicago and the Fine Arts Museums of San Francisco.

The exhibition reflects the general policy of Pope John Paul II, according to a Vatican spokesman. "Once the popes never traveled." says Walter Persegati, chief administrator of the Vatican Museums. "Christianity had to come to Rome. Now the pope goes abroad. There is a new way of interpreting the duty of a person of such responsibility. The works of art in the collection are part of this responsibility." The pope was moved by the enthusiasm of his reception during his tour of the United States in 1979, Persegati continues, and is impressed by the American determination to aid the Third World. He regards the exhibition as a gesture of understanding and encouragement for the United States to continue in the same role.

Pope John Paul II enthusiastically supports the idea that the art of the Vatican should be seen by as many people as possible. Announcing the sending of artworks to America, the pope said:

> Above all, these works of art will have a contribution to make to the men and women of our day. They will speak of history, of the human condition in its universal challenge and of the endeavors of the human spirit to attain the beauty to which it is attracted. And yes! These works of art will speak of God, because they speak of man created in the image and likeness of God; and in so many ways they will turn our attention to God Himself.

When the American exhibition was first announced, in late 1980, I had already been at work for several months on behalf of

ARTnews magazine as the first outside journalist ever admitted behind the scenes at the Vatican Museums. The backstage workings of this incomparable cultural complex were a revelation—a marvelous mosaic of art and religion in which I discovered a rich human tapestry of medieval tradition and modern management working within the walled citadel of Christian civilization.

There are, in fact, ten Vatican Museums, known officially as the Pontifical Monuments, Museums and Galleries: the Gregorian Egyptian Museum; the Gregorian Etruscan Museum; the Chiaramonti Museum and Pio-Clementine Museum (both containing classical sculpture); the Gregorian Profane Museum (classical sculpture and mosaics); the Pio Christian Museum (Early Christian inscriptions and sculpture); the Pinacoteca, or Picture Gallery (Byzantine, medieval and modern art); the Missionary-Ethnological Museum; the Collection of Modern Religious Art (the newest collection, housed in the Renaissance Borgia Apartment); and the Historical Museum (carriages and armor).

There are also several splendid chapels in addition to the Sistine Chapel (including one decorated by Fra Angelico), a loggia and apartment frescoed by Raphael, a dozen vast galleries, a library which has two museums of its own and several magnificent staircases.

This book is an attempt to share my discoveries. It is not an artwork-by-artwork guide to the Vatican Museums or to the American exhibition, though many of the works to be shown in the United States are reproduced here. It is, rather, an illustrated

Looking north from the dome of St. Peter's, Vatican landmarks are the Sistine Chapel (lower right), the Belvedere Courtyard and, behind it, the Court of the Pigna with its high, domed alcove. Beyond the garden (left) is the Pinacoteca.

"armchair tour" of what there is to see, and much that visitors never have the opportunity to see, in the Vatican Museums. I have included also highlights of my backstage experiences: surveying the Sistine Chapel from a tiny scaffold just under the ceiling with restorer Gianluigi Colalucci; examining Michelangelo's *Pietà* with the men who put it back together after a madman attacked it with a hammer; and visiting the laboratories of the men and women who preserve and restore the Vatican's treasures.

Visitors can enter the Vatican Museums through the Vatican Gardens by a special bus that runs at half-hour intervals from St. Peter's Square, but the main entrance is on the Viale Vaticano, a quarter of a mile away, through a portal dominated by statues of Michelangelo and Raphael, both by Pietro Melandri (1894–1971). In the downstairs vestibule are an information window, two spacious air-conditioned elevators with leather-upholstered benches and an electronic signboard with green, blue, yellow and red lights to signal what is open all day, half-day, part-time or not at all. On days when the Sistine Chapel is closed to the public—for the opening of a papal synod, the election of a new pope or some other event— museum attendance may drop as much as fifty percent. Recent annual attendance figures have run well over a million and a half; the relatively low figure of 1,350,000 visitors in 1978 was partly the result of the Sistine Chapel being sealed twice for the election of new popes—following the deaths of Paul VI and of his successor, John Paul I, who died after a thirty-four-day reign.

Most museum-goers resist the elevators and climb a spiraling serpentine ramp built in 1932 by Giuseppe Momo (1875–1940). Actually, there are two spirals—one for going up and the other for coming down. Their balustrade, a chronology in bronze of papal history, was designed by Antonio Maraini (1886–1963). At the top of the ramp, on a circular balcony decorated with Roman mosaics from the first to third centuries A.D., are a small Vatican post office (still the safest way to send mail out of Italy) with a writing room, souvenir counters, restrooms with water coolers, refreshment vending machines, a currency-exchange counter (Vatican rates vary slightly from, but seldom exceed, those of American Express or Roman banks) and the ticket office, over which a sign in the Vatican's five languages (English, French, German, Italian and Spanish) reads: "In paying the admission fee, you are contributing, for the pleasure of all, to the upkeep and restoration of the incomparable works of art and records of history conserved in the Vatican Museums."

Once your ticket has been taken, you will be asked to check any obtrusive or ominous-looking parcel. It is a necessary precaution, for, in one morning—not a typical one, to be sure—potentially dangerous articles discovered by security forces in bags carried by visitors included one Bowie knife, two sheath knives, one jackknife, one kitchen knife, one pair of scissors, one saw-bladed kitchen knife, five penknives and a loaded revolver. Most of these weapons were noticed in bags checked at the cloakroom, but others were intercepted in searches at the entrance turnstiles, where there is watchful scrutiny. "The gun belonged to a private detective," security chief Vittorio Rossetti recalls, "who protested that he had a permit to carry it. Of course, that was from Italy, not from the Vatican State. As one policeman to another, however, I persuaded him not to take it into the Museums, let alone the Sistine Chapel."

Once past security—which is, under the circumstances, unobtrusive—the visitor is offered a clearly mapped, color-coded choice of four routes, all starting up the grand Simonetti Stairway, built in the 1780s, with its barrel vault supported by ancient Roman columns. All four routes take in the Sistine Chapel, of course, as well as the Galleries of the Candelabra (classical sculpture), Tapestries, Maps and St. Pius V (Flemish tapestries) on the way in and the Vatican Library's Christian Museum and galleries of "minor arts" such as icons, mosaics and furniture on the way out. The purple route A, lasting an hour and a half on a leisurely stroll, is meant for visitors with little time to spare who think they want to see only the Sistine Chapel. "We can't help it," says Walter Persegati, the Vatican Museums' chief administrator, "if, coming and going, some of the beauties of our other treasures get rained upon you." The beige route B takes three hours and also includes the Borgia Apartment and Collection of Modern Religious Art, and the Etruscan, Missionary-Ethnological, Gregorian Profane, Pio Christian and Historical museums. The green route C, three and a half hours, adds to the basic purple itinerary the Rooms and Loggia (when open) of Raphael; the Egyptian, Chiaramonti and Pio-Clementine museums, plus a wing of classical sculpture, the Braccio Nuovo; Fra Angelico's chapel of Nicholas V; the Pinacoteca picture gallery; and the Library's Sistine Salon (illuminated manuscripts) and Room of the Aldobrandini Wedding (Roman frescoes). The yellow route D is the five-hour or all-day way to take in *all* the highlights of routes A, B and C, though

one is so likely to be diverted or distracted by one's own discoveries en route that it could well take five days or five weeks to "do" route D.

Today, however, we will walk directly from the first landing of the Simonetti Stairway through the first four rooms of the Pio-Clementine Museum of ancient sculptures, which the architect Michelangelo Simonetti (1724–87) created in the closing decades of the eighteenth century for Popes Clement XIV and Pius VI, after both of whom the museum is named. We will look neither right nor left as we advance resolutely upon a restful courtyard. Here we can sit on a bench and contemplate a work of art that reflects the origins and evolution of the Vatican Museums.

A wall of video monitors makes it possible for security personnel to keep a close eye on the Vatican Museums' labyrinthine galleries and corridors.

THE PIO-CLEMENTINE MUSEUM

THE VATICAN MUSEUMS originated in 1503, when Cardinal Giuliano della Rovere became Pope Julius II. From his palace near the church of San Pietro in Vincoli, the new pope brought to the Vatican an ancient statue of the god Apollo. He placed it in the inner courtyard of the Vatican's Belvedere Palace, which had been built almost two decades earlier for Innocent VIII and served as the pope's summer residence. That change of address half a millennium ago gave the statue its present name, *Apollo Belvedere*. Around it, Julius II built his Belvedere Court of the Statues and added some other sculptural treasures (*Venus Felix*, personifications of the *Nile* and the *Tiber* rivers and a *Sleeping Ariadne*).

Julius II was also responsible for the acquisition of the marble *Laocoön* group, which was unearthed in January 1506 on the Esquiline, one of the seven hills of ancient Rome. Recognized from a description by the first-century Roman writer Pliny the Elder, who preferred it to all other statues and paintings, the sculpture was purchased by Julius two months later and brought to Belvedere. In Greek mythology, Laocoön was the priest who warned the Trojans against accepting the gift horse the Greeks had carved and dedicated to the goddess Athena. His prudence angered Athena, who sent a pair of serpents to kill Laocoön and his two sons. This *Laocoön* group was carved in Rome in the first century A.D. by three sculptors from Rhodes: Hagesandros, Athanodoros and Polydoros. It shows the bearded Laocoön struggling desperately to tear away the head of the serpent biting him on the hip. The other serpent has already bitten the breast of the younger son, who is collapsing in agony, while the elder son is attempting in vain to free himself from those mortal coils.

In the late eighteenth century, this inner court—until then square in shape and planted with orange trees—was redesigned

OPPOSITE LEFT *Apollo Belvedere*, Roman copy of Greek original of the fourth century B.C., marble.
OPPOSITE RIGHT Apollonios of Athens, *Belvedere Torso*, first century B.C., marble.

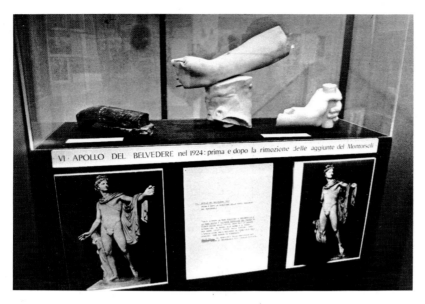

ABOVE Display showing the *Apollo Belvedere* before and after the removal in 1924 of Montorsoli's restorations.
OPPOSITE Hagesandros, Polydoros and Athanodoros of Rhodes, *Laocoön*, first century A.D., marble.

by Simonetti into what is now the inviting Octagonal Court of the Pio-Clementine Museum. In the early nineteenth century, Pope Pius VII bought three splendid statues by Antonio Canova and placed them in the court: *Perseus*, triumphant with the head of Medusa, and the boxers *Kreugas* and *Damoxenos* confronting each other.

Of all the great works of art occupying niches under the eight-sided portico that surrounds a leafy goldfish pond where tourists like to picnic, the *Apollo Belvedere* was and is the first. And, when one looks into the *Apollo*'s eyes, which the German Romantic poet Friedrich Hölderlin said "observe with silent, eternal light," or at the incomplete whole which Johann Joachim Winckelmann, the German art historian who was commissioner of antiquities of the Papal States from 1763 to 1768, called "the highest ideal of art," one is confronting the very heart of the Vatican Museums.

The *Apollo Belvedere* is believed to be a Roman copy in marble from the second century A.D. of a Greek bronze from the fourth century B.C. The lost original, probably by Leochares, once stood in the agora of Athens. The Roman copy is not exact, and neither is the date when it resurfaced in Italy sometime in the fourteenth century with both hands missing. The earliest known written mention of it dates back to 1491, a dozen years before Pope Julius II brought it to the Vatican.

In 1532, Pope Clement VII commissioned Giovanni Angelo da Montorsoli to reconstruct both the *Laocoön* (his right arm was missing) and the *Apollo Belvedere*. Taking his cue from mythology and other Greek statues of Apollo, Montorsoli not only gave the god ("he who strikes from afar") new hands, but also put a bow in his left hand and an arrow in his right hand. Surgically and cosmetically, Montorsoli did a beautiful job, but the patient might have had cause for complaint, because Montorsoli sawed off and threw away much of what was left of the *Apollo*'s right arm and some of his left arm in order to attach whole

Boy with Goose, Roman copy of Greek original of the third to second century B.C., marble.

Eros of Centocelle, Roman copy of Greek original of the fourth century B.C., marble.

new forearms with hands. And, although one could tell from the position of the original arms that the god's right hand faced inward to rest against his right thigh, Montorsoli had the right hand open outward. Then he enlarged the tree stump beneath and behind the right forearm so it would support the right hand.

The nineteenth-century era of great excavations in the Egyptian, Etruscan, Greek and Roman worlds led to a new regard for the integrity of original works and a respect even for fragments. It was no longer regarded as desirable to give old statues new limbs. In 1905, a German archeologist named Ludwig Pollak discovered the missing right arm of *Laocoön* in a Roman marble-cutter's shop, and it was placed on the statue in a later restoration, but a plaster cast of Montorsoli's previous restoration is also preserved in the Octagonal Court as part of the *Laocoön* group's history.

In 1924, at the zenith of the new purism, the *Apollo Belvedere*'s turn for therapy came. The first archeologist to serve as Vatican Museums director-general, Bartolomeo Nogara, decreed, and restorer Guido Galli executed, the removal of the Montorsoli embellishments from the *Apollo Belvedere*. Away went the artificial forearms and hands. The god was disarmed, too, of bow and arrow. But now, with no hands and no tree stump to rest his arm stump upon, the *Apollo Belvedere* was in danger of keeling over. So two iron rods, one rising up from the pedestal and the other reaching out from the wall niche to support the statue's shoulders, were attached from behind to keep the figure stable. Recently, however, after standing outdoors for more than half a century, those rods were rusting and threatening to discolor the figure they were supposed to enhance.

The expert whose responsibilities include restoration and preservation of the *Apollo*

Bust of Pericles, Roman copy of Greek original by Cresilas, fifth century B.C., marble.

Belvedere is Dr. Georg Daltrop, who was appointed curator of classical art in the Vatican Museums in 1967 at the age of thirty-five. The German-born academician, formerly a curator of antiquities in West Germany, holds degrees from the Universities of Munich and Münster and is fluent in five languages. His linguistic ability does not deter Daltrop from remarking wistfully that he would much prefer to have all the inscriptions and labels in his domain "just in Latin, because that's so much clearer and more direct, don't you think?"

Considering the iron supporting rods of the *Apollo Belvedere*, Daltrop remarks that they were doubly destructive. "First of all, fastening the *Apollo* to the wall with that heavy iron clamp meant that the public couldn't see him from the back. A sculpture is three-dimensional and meant for people to go all around it, not for them to see it from the front like a painting." Second and most offensive of all to Daltrop were the clean-cut surgical stumps of the *Apollo*'s arms, resulting from Montorsoli's work: "If they were broken off the way they were found, that would have been fine. But your fantasy is outraged when you see cut hands."

In 1974–75, Daltrop took four months off from his duties to ponder the *Apollo Belvedere*'s problems at Princeton University's Institute for Advanced Study. There he came up with two possible solutions that would allow him to remove the iron rods before they did any real harm.

The first solution would have been to replace the false hands and tree stump that the god had used for almost four centuries: "Anything is better than what he has now,"

The Belvedere Court of Pope Julius II was incorporated into the Octagonal Court of the Pio-Clementine Museum in 1773 by architect Michelangelo Simonetti.

said Daltrop. The second was to restore the figure to its pre-Montorsoli appearance, which we know from a drawing in the 1491 *Codex Escurialensis*, a sketchbook from the school of Ghirlandaio. "Restoring it this way would be no major problem," says Daltrop. "Sixty years ago, it may not have been feasible, but nowadays it is not impossibly difficult to stabilize a slightly broken statue so that it can stand on its own. We have enough experience to do it."

Daltrop leaned toward the second solution and said the major remaining questions involved "organizing the specialists" to do the job without taking the *Apollo* off public view any longer than necessary. But one hesitates to tamper, even for the better, with so famous and important a work of art. Other developments, too, added uncertainty as to which approach (or mixture of both) to take. For example, in a 1954 excavation in Baia, near Naples, an impression of a hand was found. After using the impression to make a plaster cast, which he keeps in his office, Daltrop decided that it would match up almost perfectly with the presumed position

The Rotunda Room was designed by Simonetti in imitation of the Pantheon. Among the Roman statues in niches around the perimeter is a colossal gilded-bronze *Hercules* leaning on his club. The floor mosaics, showing battles between Greeks and centaurs and mythical sea beasts disporting with nereids and tritons, once decorated the Baths of Otricoli. The huge porphyry basin in the center of the room comes from Nero's palace.

of the *Apollo*'s left hand. So then Daltrop had to decide whether to rebuild the left forearm and hand accordingly. And he also had to decide whether to return the right forearm to its 1491 (handless) condition, or to add the original inward-turned hand that can be deduced by the position of the broken arm, or to replace the outward-stretched hand that had been created by Montorsoli.

Early in 1981, a wooden wall sealed off the *Apollo*'s niche in the Octagonal Court from public view. Behind the barriers, the chief sculpture restorer of the Vatican Museums, Ulderico Grispigni, and two assistants prepared the statue for surgery. First, with supporting rods and fig leaf removed, they made a paster-cast copy of the *Apollo Belvedere* to remain behind when the sculpture embarked upon its first transatlantic trip: to the United States for the 1983 exhibition. (One condition of Vatican loan policies is that a perfect copy of each outgoing sculpture must be made at the expense of the borrower.) Another presurgical decision had also been taken: not to do anything about the hands until after the statue comes back from New York, since no unanimous plan of action had been reached by Daltrop, Vatican Museums Director-General Carlo Pietrangeli and the five other curators of the Vatican Museums at their periodic restoration conferences. Surgery can be a drastic and dangerous cure, as the *Apollo* already knows too well.

When the plaster cast was ready, it was placed on display and the original was removed to the Vatican Museums scientific laboratories for X-ray analysis. Chemical stabilizers had been prepared for injection through microtubes into the existing holes. And a special drill had been custom-designed in Italy that allowed Grispigni to work from all angles with a minimum of vibration.

The job took less than six months, and as it

Thalia, Roman copy of Greek original of the second century B.C., marble.

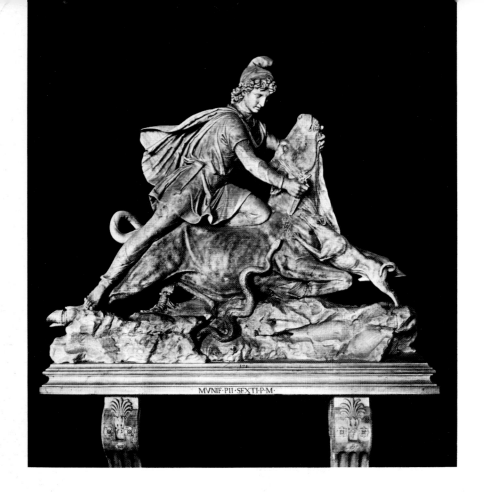

turned out, no chemicals were necessary. By replacing the corrodible iron rods inside the *Apollo* with Teflon-shielded stainless steel mini-rods in a different pattern of connections created by Grispigni's delicate drilling, which was minimal, and by shifting the statue's stance on its stone base by five centimeters (not quite two inches), the sculpture was stabilized and the *Apollo Belvedere* enabled to stand on its own two feet. He was placed back on public view in March 1982.

Walking back to the Simonetti Stairway from the Octagonal Court, we pause this time before the *Belvedere Torso* in the Pio-Clementine's Room of the Muses. Known to have been in the collection of Cardinal Colonna in the 1430s, it came to the Vatican early in the sixteenth century. Headless, armless, legless from the knees down, this larger-than-life neo-Attic sculpture from the first century B.C. is yet one of the most influential works of art in history.

On the rock upon which the figure rests is carved, as clear as yesterday's graffiti, the signature "Apollonios, son of Nestor, Athenian, made it." The *Torso* is leaning forward and to the left. Little is known about its subject, but it is eloquent in the language of form. Michelangelo admired it greatly and is quoted as saying: "This is the work of a man who knew more than nature; it is a great misfortune that it is lost [broken]." It is said that Michelangelo learned anatomy by constant study of the *Belvedere Torso*, and its lessons are realized in the Sistine Chapel's *Last Judgment*, in the postures of many of the damned in descent as well as that of St. Bartholomew holding a human skin.

The impact of these three sculptures—the *Apollo Belvedere*, the *Laocoön* group and the *Belvedere Torso*—upon the greatness of the Vatican Museums might even be termed eternal. By 1514, Julius II's successor, Leo X

ABOVE *Calliope*, Roman copy of Greek original of the second century B.C., marble.
OPPOSITE ABOVE *Mithras*, second century A.D., marble.
OPPOSITE BELOW *Triton with Nereid and Cupids*, first century B.C., marble.

(Giovanni de' Medici, son of Lorenzo the Magnificent), was defining the study of antiquity as "the finest and most useful task that God could assign to mortals, after that of knowing Him and preserving the true faith. This study refines and beautifies our existence . . . and helps us in the most various circumstances: salutary in adversity, fitting and decorous in favorable circumstances, so much so that without it every human interest seems to lose its solidity, and no pleasure in civil society seems to be able in any way to exist." A few years later, another Medici pope, Clement VII (who was Leo X's cousin Giulio de' Medici), heeded the message and continued the tradition by purchasing the *Torso*, possibly from the widow of the sculptor and collector Andrea Bregno, and placing it in the Belvedere Court of the Statues. Years later, it was moved indoors to an adjacent vestibule, which in modern times proved too small and congested for safety and viewing. In 1973 it was made the centerpiece in the Room of the Muses.

This room takes its name from sculptures of seven of the muses found in 1774 at the Villa of Brutus near Tivoli. They date from the second century A.D. A noble herm-pillar bearing a bust is a monument to Pericles, the Athenian statesman and general, who is also identified on the inscription as the son of Xanthippos. He is wearing a Corinthian helmet signifying his rank of *strategòs*, commander-in-chief of the army. This stone herm is a Roman Imperial Age copy of a Greek original made by the sculptor Cresilas immediately after Pericles perished in the plague of 429 B.C.

In the Pio-Clementine's nearby Gallery of

LEFT *Venus of Cnidos*, Roman copy of Greek original by Praxiteles, fourth century B.C., marble.
OPPOSITE *Mattei Amazon*, Roman copy of Greek original by Cresilas, fifth century B.C., marble.

Statues is another Roman copy of a Greek original, the *Eros of Centocelle*, its wings long-missing. The original was of the Peloponnesian school of the fourth century B.C.

In the Gallery of Statues are also such treasured Roman copies of lost Greek originals as the *Apollo Sauroktonos* ("he who kills the lizard"), based on a sculpture of the

OPPOSITE *Funerary Monument to M. Gratidius Libanus and Gratidia M. L. Carite*, Roman, first century B.C., marble.

BELOW *Sleeping Ariadne*, Roman copy of Greek original of the second century B.C., marble. Serving as a base is a sarcophagus of the second century A.D. carved with a battle between gods and giants with serpent-like legs.

fourth century B.C. by Praxiteles. It represents the god—arrow in hand and an almost girlish expression on his face—preparing to spear a lizard that is climbing up a tree trunk. The *Mattei Amazon*, whose left thigh is wounded, is a Roman copy of a fifth-century B.C. original by Cresilas. A statue of a sleeping woman was once believed to represent Cleopatra because her armlet was thought to be an asp, but was later labeled *Sleeping Ariadne*. Abandoned on the island of Naxos by the Athenian warrior Theseus, whom she had helped to kill the Minotaur, she awaits the coming of her future husband, Dionysos, the god of wine. A particularly admired copy of a Hellenistic period (second-century B.C.) original, the *Sleeping Ariadne* was one of the first statues with which Julius II embellished his Belvedere Court.

While the contents of the Pio-Clementine's Room of the Animals date from the fourth century B.C. to the fourth century A.D., most of the works were so radically restored by Francesco Antonio Franzoni (1734–1818) that they may now almost be credited to him. Its most important piece is a larger-than-life statue of the great hunter *Meleager* with his

dog and the head of a boar he has killed. Carved in second-century Rome, it was based upon an original attributed to Scopas, one of the greatest Greek sculptors of the fourth century B.C. But this busy room's exuberant delight is a virtuoso fountain of a triton carrying off a bare-breasted, leggy sea nymph while two cupids hitch a ride by clinging to the triton's tail. One cupid holds finger to mouth as if shushing the beauty who protests only a little too much; the other, cupping hand to ear, is happily feigning sympathy. There is a hole between the triton's legs from which the fountain's water used to spring. Installed on any piazza in Rome today, it would be a tourist attraction to compete with the Trevi Fountain. It dates from the first century B.C. and represents a late, "rococo" stage of Hellenistic art.

In the Pio-Clementine Room of the Busts there is a relief from a Roman funerary monument of the first century B.C. showing a mature couple holding hands. An inscription (now lost) identified them as "M. Gratidius Libanus and Gratidia M. L. Carite," but to everyone from curators to cleaners in the Vatican Museums they are known fondly as

Cato and Portia. The couple's right hands are joined in the wedding gesture of faith and concord, which they are repeating in the face of death as a sign of eternal union.

In the Cabinet of the Masks (named after its floor mosaics of theatrical masks), the *Venus of Cnidos* has taken off her robe and is placing it over a vase as she prepares for her bath. It is a Roman copy of another great work by Praxiteles: a cult statue made in the fourth century B.C. for a shrine on the Greek peninsula of Cnidos (now in southwestern Turkey). According to Pliny, people flocked from all over the world to see this famous beauty. It was the first cult statue in which the goddess of love appeared in the nude.

The great architect Michelangelo Simonetti laid out a variety of rooms along the route from his Stairway to his Octagonal Court. The Greek Cross Room, with four arms of equal length, offers a dignified, symmetrical setting for two monumental sarcophagi of dark red Egyptian porphyry. One belonged to Constance, daughter of the Emperor Constantine, and the other belonged to his mother, St. Helena, who was converted to Christianity in A.D. 313, the year Constantine legalized the religion. While the daughter's sarcophagus shows cupids, peacocks and a ram, her grandmother's is decorated on all four sides with high reliefs of victorious Roman cavaliers trampling prostrate chained barbarians. Since this seems an unlikely subject for the sarcophagus of a pious woman of royal rank, it is possible that this one was originally made for Constantine himself before his conversion.

Simonetti's masterpiece is his domed Pantheon-inspired Rotunda Room, seventy-one feet in diameter and seventy-two feet high at the cupola. Its treasures include the colossal head of the *Jupiter of Otricoli*, a Roman version of a famous Greek statue of Zeus of the fourth century B.C., and a monumental gilded-bronze statue of *Hercules* from the late second century A.D. that was discovered in 1864 near Pompey's Theatre, the first stone theatre built in Rome (it lasted from 52 B.C. to the sixth century A.D.). The statue had been carefully buried and the letters "F.C.S." inscribed on the slabs of stone covering it. These initials stood for *Fulgor Conditum Summanium*, indicating that the statue had been struck by lightning and buried on the spot.

What strikes the eye first, though, in this room are the Roman statues in niches circling a floor decorated with ancient mosaics from Otricoli: scenes of battle between Greeks and centaurs, and mythical marine animals making merry with mermaids and mermen. Its centerpiece is a huge red basin from the Domus Aurea, or Golden House, the lavish palace that Nero built for himself. Forty-three feet in circumference, the bowl was carved from a single block of porphyry. If the total effect is dazzling, the glory goes to the architect who arranged it all, Michelangelo Simonetti.

In recent decades, the mosaic floor of Simonetti's rotunda has seldom been seen intact, for much of it has been carpeted over. When people were allowed to walk on it, whether in high or low heels, their footsteps detached the tesserae (little cubes of mosaic), and a restorer used to work full-time just to preserve the cubes and put them back in place. But now the Vatican Museums' chief scientist, Nazzareno Gabrielli, can report hopefully: "Over the past few years, we've been working on the mosaics, using substances similar to what preserves marble nowadays, and we've managed to consolidate them so that now they're stabilized." Gabrielli promises that the rug will someday be removed and the mosaic will be visible again.

ABOVE *Jupiter of Otricoli*, Roman copy of Greek original
of the fourth century B.C., marble.
RIGHT Antonio Canova, *Kreugas*, 1802, marble.

THE CHIARAMONTI MUSEUM AND THE BRACCIO NUOVO

FOR POPE JULIUS II, MICHELANGELO'S patron, the architect Donato Bramante (1444–1514) designed a splendid entrance into the Belvedere Palace. The Bramante Stairway was built in the early sixteenth century so that cavaliers, including the dashing Pope Julius himself, could enter on horseback from the Vatican Gardens. A cobblestoned spiraling ramp, it anticipated Frank Lloyd Wright's Guggenheim Museum by four and a half centuries, but it is built within an oblong tower, and in accordance with the principles enunciated by the Roman architect Vitruvius around the time of Christ, Bramante built the columns in three different styles: Tuscan (a simplified Doric) at the bottom, Ionic as one ascends and Corinthian at the top.

Near the base of this tower is the Fountain of the Galleon, a lovely lead boat whose cannon spout water. It looks like one of Columbus's vessels and it is only a little more recent than the *Niña*, the *Pinta* and the *Santa Maria*. Made by Carlo Maderno (1556–1629) for Pope Paul V, who reigned at the beginning of the seventeenth century, the fountain was not installed here until the papacy of Clement IX in the late 1660s. Even more distracting than the fountain below is the grand view of Rome from every window as one walks along the tower's cobblestones, where human feet clatter like the cavalry that hasn't been heard here for centuries. Most distracting of all, though, is the hypnotic view down the deep inner well, which is why the Bramante Stairway is closed to the public (though scholars and art historians may see it by applying in advance). As administrator Persegati explains, "It's so easy for a child to fall into that hole. In fact, spaces between the banister rods are so wide that even an adult could fall in. Historically and artistically, the Bramante Stairway is so important that you can't just put chicken wire in between. We have in mind to put in plate glass to protect the center, but it's a huge and expensive proposition to do the whole job. But, until nobody can fall in, we can't risk keeping it open because it's too

OPPOSITE *Funerary Stele for a Young Man*, Greek, ca. 450 B.C., marble.

tempting just to peer over and look down, down, down."

The hand and image of Donato Bramante recur throughout the early history of the Vatican Museums. Raphael used a Bramante design for a basilica in his fresco *The School of Athens* in the apartment he decorated for Julius II. Having succeeded Bramante as chief architect of the Vatican, Raphael also inherited the task of decorating the loggia overlooking the Courtyard of St. Damasus. In the Borgia Apartment's Room of the Liberal Arts, the lunette figure of Euclid is believed to be a portrait of Bramante, perhaps by Pinturicchio. And on the Sistine Chapel ceiling, Michelangelo's prophet Joel, perusing a parchment, is presumed also to be a portrait of Bramante. It is said that Bramante, no friend of Michelangelo's, was the one who, in 1508, suggested his young rival to Julius II for the suicidal mission of decorating the Sistine celing with something more elaborate than the simple starry sky painted by Pier Matteo d'Amelia a quarter of a century earlier. If so, we owe much to Bramante's envy.

Though they lived more than three centuries apart, Bramante and Antonio Canova (1757–1822), the sculptor who became the first full-time director-general of the Vatican Museums in 1805, work together —not far from the Octagonal Court and Bramante Stairway—in a corridor that Bramante built to connect the Papal Palace with the Belvedere summer residence. Canova decorated it with statuary, and in 1807 it became the Chiaramonti Museum, named after its founder, Barnaba Chiaramonti, who reigned as Pope Pius VII from 1800 to 1823 and for whom Canova

journeyed to Paris in 1815 to arrange and supervise the return of the Pio-Clementine art treasures that had been taken to France by Napoleon.

A long hall devoted to ancient sculpture, the Chiaramonti Museum is lined with busts, statues of gods, pagan altars, urns and sarcophagi: 976 objects are displayed along its awesome length. By the time the museum was a quarter of a century old, an author of the time, Erasmo Pistolesi, had written, "Indeed the things to be seen in the long corridor are so numerous that, instead of soothing the spirit, they put it in turmoil."

Bramante's corridor continues with the adjoining Lapidary Gallery of Early Christian inscriptions on one wall and pagan inscriptions (by emperors, consuls, magistrates and other officials, plus a more recent No Smoking sign) on the opposite wall.

Perpendicular to Bramante's corridor is the Braccio Nuovo, or New Wing, a much more austere Neoclassical hall designed in the early nineteenth century by the Roman architect Raffaele Stern. Ancient statues fill the niches: the Greek orator *Demosthenes*, a *Wounded Amazon*, a *Colossus of the Nile* and several Roman emperors, all flanking a mosaic floor depicting the adventures of Ulysses, taken from a Roman villa of the second century A.D. One of the most notable Braccio Nuovo statues is the heroic *Augustus of Prima Porta*, considered the best portrait extant of the first Roman emperor, who lived from 63 B.C. to A.D. 14. He is shown around the age of forty, barefoot, with his right arm raised. Since the emperor is wearing armor, we may assume he is addressing his troops. The relief decorations on his breastplate are considered as fine as the portrait itself. The central scene shows the Parthian king, Phrates IV, returning the Roman insignia (lost in 53 B.C.)

OPPOSITE *Augustus of Prima Porta* (detail), Roman, probably a copy commissioned by the emperor's wife, Livia, after his death in A.D. 14, of an original made ca. 20 B.C., marble.

to Tiberius, Augustus's deputy, in 20 B.C. The whole cosmos witnesses the peace offering: Sky with billowing cloak; Sun riding a four-horse chariot; personifications of Dawn, Dew and Fertility; Apollo with his lyre, riding a winged griffin; and Diana bearing a flaming torch, on a stag. This scene is flanked by two seated female figures personifying provinces, possibly Germania and Dacia. The right leg of Augustus rests upon a cupid riding a dolphin—a reference to the fabled ancestral descent from Venus of the Julian family, to which Augustus (a grandson of Julius Caesar's sister) belonged.

This figure of the emperor was found in 1863 at the Villa of Livia, Augustus's wife, at Prima Porta on the via Flaminia. It is probably a copy, commissioned by the widow immediately after his death, of a bronze statue erected in honor of Augustus around 20 B.C. Of historical interest is the sculptor's portrait of Tiberius, Livia's son by her first marriage, as his stepfather's deputy in the central scene, though Tiberius would have been only thirteen at the time and scarcely in such a position of power. But it constitutes the first official recognition of Tiberius as his stepfather's successor.

Squeezed between the Gregorian Egyptian Museum and the Stairway of the Assyrian Reliefs are the Rooms of the Greek Originals: two rooms and an art-lined corridor, all with fifth- and fourth-century B.C. fragments of statues and reliefs that had been, until 1960, mixed up with Roman originals and copies either in the galleries or the warehouse. Among the notable Greek originals are a larger-than-life marble head of a goddess

Colossus of the Nile, Roman copy of Greek original, marble.

Antonio Canova, *Portrait Bust of Pope Pius VII*, 1820-22, marble. Pius VII was the founder of the Braccio Nuovo.

render so clearly the sense of a young life brought to an end," Daltrop says, "belonged only to the dawn of classical Greek art, around 450 B.C." Though this relief was known to have stood in a Roman villa in the sixteenth century, it disappeared from sight for almost four hundred years—until 1902, when its upper part, slightly incomplete, was found in a Roman church, where its lower part was also discovered forty-eight years later.

Achilles as Doryphoros, Roman copy of Greek original by Polyclitus, fifth century B.C., marble.

with inlaid gray stone eyes, bronze-leaf eyebrows, pierced ears and holes drilled in her head to hold a missing helmet. Since the only female deity allowed to wear a helmet was Athena, we can presume it is she. In the same room is a fragment of a relief depicting a serene horseman riding a restless steed. It recalls the horseman frieze of the Parthenon in Athens, though it cannot be from there because it is of a different marble. The other Room of the Greek Originals, however, is entirely devoted to fragments from or pertaining to the Parthenon. And the corridor offers a full view of the large funerary stele (commemorative slab) for a youth, shown standing thoughtfully with head bowed and left arm raised in greeting. A fragmentary servent boy is offering him a round ointment jar with one hand and, with the other, a *strigil*, the cliplike instrument which athletes used to rub dust and sweat off their skin after sports. "The capacity to

THE PINACOTECA

THE RECTANGULAR BRICK Pinacoteca, or Picture Gallery, is a formal but friendly building crowned by white chess-piece swirls above gold mosaics inlaid with the names of some of the famous artists whose paintings hang inside. Waiting for us here is a bearded man in his forties who looks like a jaunty schoolteacher. He is Dr. Fabrizio Mancinelli, who in 1972 became Vatican Museums curator of Byzantine, medieval and modern art. He was thirty-two then and is still the youngest of the six curators, but he presides over the longest time span—thirteen centuries, from the fifth through the eighteenth. "Here," Mancinelli says, "by modern art we mean a period dating from the discovery of America to the end of the eighteenth century. You must not confuse *modern* with *contemporary*."

Though his domain includes the Sistine Chapel, the Raphael Rooms and Loggia as well as the Renaissance walls and trappings of many of the other curators' galleries (including the Borgia Apartment), Mancinelli has elected to join us here at the Pinacoteca, which was inaugurated by Pius XI in 1932. That pope is honored by a bust in the vestibule; at present, there are only two other sculptures (fourteenth-century refugees from St. Peter's) on display in a building consecrated primarily to paintings. In stately and orderly fashion, mostly chronologically, the Pinacoteca displays the last eight of Mancinelli's thirteen centuries.

In the first room, Mancinelli points with the tip of an unlit pipe to a speck of blue in the corner over the halo of a twelfth-century religious panel and remarks that we are witnessing something of a miracle, for all the other blues around it long ago turned black or brown with age. "The sky was blue in those days," he says, "and now it looks like today's skies."

A large fan-shaped *Last Judgment*, painted in tempera on a wood panel, is better preserved. The work of two artists, Giovanni

OPPOSITE Barocci, *The Rest on the Flight into Egypt*, ca. 1573, oil on canvas.

and Niccolo, of the late eleventh and early twelfth centuries, this is one of the grandest of Italian primitive paintings. It was commissioned by two Benedictine nuns, who are depicted at bottom left (the Paradise corner of the predella), four levels beneath Christ, who is riding a rainbow. This altarpiece envisions a more stately doomsday than Michelangelo's in the Sistine Chapel.

Also in the first room is a tempera-on-wood *St. Francis of Assisi*, one of the earliest representations of the saint, who died in 1226 and was canonized two years later, painted by Margaritone di Arezzo (1216–93).

In the second room, the centerpiece is the *Stefaneschi Polyptych*, painted about 1315 by Giotto and his assistants for Cardinal Jacopo Gaetani Stefaneschi, who is depicted twice therein: in the front central panel he is kneeling by Christ's right foot; in the back central panel he is donating the polyptych to St. Peter, and, in fact, the polyptych was kept in the Basilica of St. Peter from Giotto's time until 1931. In its front left panel, we see the crucifixion of St. Peter, hanging head downward. He has just died and angels are carrying his soul to God. Giotto's angels' wings, incidentally, match their robes—green on green, pink on pink. In the front right panel, St. Paul has just been beheaded and his soul, too, is being carried to heaven by Giotto's immaculate angels. Giotto, like Dante, came to Rome as a pilgrim in the Holy Year of 1300 and is mentioned in *The Divine Comedy* for having displaced Cimabue as the foremost painter of the time. Two side panels of the predella have been lost.

In the same room is *The Vision of St. Thomas Aquinas*, an exquisitely simple panel of a polyptych painted by Sassetta between 1423 and 1426.

Room three features a large Filippo Lippi triptych of the *Coronation of the Virgin*, painted around 1460 on a commission from Carlo Marsuppini, secretary of the Republic of Florence, who is shown kneeling in the left panel. But this room is known as the Room of Fra Angelico, for there are no fewer than four of his panels from the 1430s: *Madonna and Child with St. Dominic, St. Catherine and Angels* and *St. Francis Receiving the Stigmata* as well as two larger *Episodes from the Life of St. Nicholas of Bari*. All are resplendent in luminous colors, with red and blue predominating; the contrasts in *St. Francis* are almost awesome. Fra Angelico's prized pupil and collaborator, Benozzo Gozzoli (1420–97), is represented on the opposite wall by the *Madonna of the Sash*, a tempera-on-wood altarpiece with a sliding panel (beneath the Virgin's feet) used for communicating with nuns in seclusion.

Some panels in the first three rooms have gaping scars with bare wood showing beneath the missing flesh of saints and martyrs. "This is what we call 'archeological restoration,'" Mancinelli explains, defining his term succinctly as "to leave missing what is missing." But, on the fourth in a series of *Opere della Misericordia* from the Scuola Marchigiana (medieval artists from the Marches area of east-central Italy), "the missing pieces have been replaced because all the other panels were in perfect condition and we wanted the whole effect to have integrity. Do you see the stripes on the red bedspread? They are restoration. And it is not bad restoration just because you can see it. Everything we make new must be detectable: that is the rule of what we call 'integral restoration.' So, if you look from a normal distance, you don't see the stripes, but if you peer close, you do."

The first three rooms, Mancinelli explains, were "very different" when he first arrived. He eliminated everything that wasn't medieval and made other arrangements (a new room has been built) for an extensive

ABOVE *The Prophet Amos*, ca. 1120–30, fresco fragment.
RIGHT Margaritone d'Arezzo, *St. Francis of Assisi*, ca.
1270–80, panel.

ABOVE Sassetta, *The Vision of St. Thomas Aquinas,*
1423–26, predella panel.
OPPOSITE Giotto and assistants, *Stefaneschi Polyptych,*
ca. 1315. ABOVE *Christ in Majesty,* front central panel.
BELOW *Madonna in Majesty,* predella panel.

Gentile da Fabriano, *Episodes from the Life of St. Nicholas of Bari*, 1425, predella panels: ABOVE *St. Nicholas Bestowing a Dowry of Golden Balls on Three Poor Maidens*. BELOW *St. Nicholas Saving a Ship from a Storm at Sea*.

Fra Angelico, *Episodes from the Life of St. Nicholas of Bari*, 1437, predella panels. ABOVE *Birth of St. Nicholas, His Vocation and Bestowing a Dowry of Golden Balls.* BELOW *St. Nicholas Saving His City from Famine and Saving a Ship from a Storm at Sea.*

ABOVE Perugino, *Madonna and Child with Four Saints*,
1495, panel.
OPPOSITE LEFT Fra Angelico, *St. Lawrence Receiving the
Treasure of the Church from Pope Sixtus II* (detail),
fresco in the Chapel of Nicholas V, 1447–50.
OPPOSITE RIGHT Melozzo da Forlì, *Angel Making Music*,
ca. 1480, fresco fragment.

collection of Byzantine icons that used to be sandwiched in chronologically. And he took most of the isolated panels from triptychs and polyptychs out of their gold frames "because this technique of displaying them made them look like single self-contained whole pieces while I wanted to show them as fragments of a whole."

The fourth room is dominated by a Melozzo da Forlì (1438–94) fresco that was on a Vatican Library wall for more than four centuries before being detached and transferred to canvas. Painted in 1477, it shows Pope Sixtus IV, who had the Sistine Chapel built and from whom it takes it name, approving the nomination of a kneeling Bartolomeo Secchi, known as Platina, to be the first prefect of the Vatican Library in 1475. The appointment of Platina, a noted biographer of the popes, marked the official beginning of the Vatican Library as decreed by a Papal Bull of June 15, 1475. The cardinal standing before the pudgy pope is his nephew, Giuliano della Rovere, who, more than thirty years later, as Pope Julius II, put Michelangelo to work in his uncle's chapel.

"Transferring frescoes from walls onto canvas," says Mancinelli, "is one of the riskiest tasks in the world of art. Fortunately, we get the frescoes only *after* they've been removed, and the rest is difficult but not dangerous." Although this room also features a Marco Palmezzano (1459–1539) tempera-on-wood *Madonna and Child with Saints*, it could still be called the Melozzo Room, for it displays a dozen fragments of this very rare but always exquisite Umbrian painter's earthy *Apostles* and heavenly *Angels Making Music*. Melozzo was noted for the loving detail and accuracy with which he painted each and every musical instrument.

Room five is devoted to "fifteen various fifteenth-century painters," all but one Italian, creating Madonnas and miracles. The foreigner is Lucas Cranach the Elder, whose rugged and harsh Germanic *Pietà* looks as colorful as, but much more clinical than, its neighbors.

The sixth room of the Pinacoteca is filled with massive golden polyptychs, of which the most complex is *St. Anthony Abbot with Other Saints* by Antonio Vivarini, who signed and dated it in 1469. Vivarini grouped nine painted panels around a wooden statue of St. Anthony holding a gilded pike symbolizing his advanced age: he died in a cave near the Red Sea around the age of 100. St. Anthony Abbot, the founder of monasticism, forsook his wealthy family in Egypt to live in a ruin near the Nile and overcome all weaknesses of the flesh.

Room seven is labeled "Fifteenth Century Umbrian School" and features two Pinturicchios, *Coronation of the Virgin* and *Madonna and Child*, as well as four Peruginos: *Madonna and Child with Four Saints* and portraits of *St. Flavia*, *St. Placido* and *St. Benedict*. Mancinelli points out a pallid Giovanni Santi tempera-on-canvas *St. Jerome Enthroned*. "Not one of his masterpieces," he remarks. Then why are we looking at it? "Because his son, Raphael Sanzio, is waiting for you in the next room."

The domed eighth room of the Pinacoteca is indeed *the* Raphael room, not to be confused with the Raphael Rooms *(Stanze di Raffaello)* near the Sistine Chapel. Here, at the hub of the fifteen-room Pinacoteca, three large altarpieces line one wall: *The Coronation of the Virgin*, the *Madonna of Foligno* and the monumental *Transfiguration*. The predella, or base, of

OPPOSITE Leonardo da Vinci, *St. Jerome in the Wilderness*, ca. 1480, panel.

49

LEFT AND BELOW Perugino, *St. Benedict* and *St. Placidus*, 1496–98, panels from a larger composition.
OPPOSITE Raphael, *Madonna of Foligno*, ca. 1512, panel, transferred to canvas.

50

The Coronation of the Virgin is displayed under glass.

In *The Coronation of the Virgin* (1503), Christ is receiving his mother and crowning her Queen of Heaven, while, down on earth, Saints Thomas, Peter, Paul and John, among others, bear witness at her graveside. Every face, every robe, every angel in the choir, every instrument was exquisitely drawn—serene and lovely and loving—by the twenty-year-old Raphael with a brilliance of detail that even Melozzo might envy.

In a case before the *Madonna of Foligno* lies a second Raphael predella that is part of another picture and period. Sometimes listed as the *Predella of the Borghese Deposition* because it belonged to Raphael's *Descent from the Cross* in Rome's Borghese Gallery, it is known in the Vatican as the *Baglioni Predella* because Raphael painted it for Atalanta Baglioni to honor her son after he was killed in Perugia in 1507. At that time, young Raphael was still under the influence of Michelangelo, so his depiction of the Theological Virtues—Faith, Hope and Charity—is severe and uniform, seemingly monochromatic and sculptural.

The cherub-clouded *Madonna of Foligno* was commissioned about 1512 by Sigismondo de' Conti, Pope Julius II's friend and chamberlain, who is shown kneeling in front of St. Jerome and giving thanks to the Virgin that a thunderbolt which had struck Conti's house in Foligno had caused no damage. A wooden tablet held by one cherub is bare. It was intended for a written account of the event, but the donor died before it could be added. The bare wood reminds us that Raphael originally painted the *Madonna of Foligno* on wood, but it was transferred to canvas in 1801 during its stay in Paris, where it had been taken by Napoleon. It is considered representative of Raphael's second period when, having freed himself from the influence of Michelangelo, he turned toward a more Venetian, less linear way of painting.

What makes this room of rooms Raphael's shrine is the altarpiece that is the centerpiece and masterpiece of its wall of paintings: the oil-on-wood *Transfiguration* (1517–20). It was his last work, the magnificent manifesto of the master's style in his final years. When Raphael died on his thirty-seventh birthday at Eastertime in 1520, it was not quite completed, and the chronicler Vasari recounts that "they placed at his head, in the room where he worked, the painting of the Transfiguration . . . and, on seeing the body dead and the painting full of life, the hearts of all who looked at it overflowed with grief. . . . It seems that he so concentrated his strength to show the force and skill of art in the face of Christ that, when it was finished, as if that were the last thing he had to do, he did not touch a brush again, and death came to him."

Raphael painted Christ appearing to Saints Peter, James and John (and, on the side, Saints Julian and Lawrence) on Mount Tabor in much the manner described in Matthew 17: " . . . and was transfigured before them; and his face did shine as the sun, and his raiment was white as the light. And behold, there appeared unto them Moses and Elijah talking with him." The other apostles are waiting anxiously at the foot of Mount Tabor, where a boy possessed of the devil is causing concern and anguish. Completed by Raphael's pupils Giulio Romano (ca. 1499–1546) and Giovan Francesco Penni (ca. 1488–1528), the *Transfiguration* represents a transcendence for the artist himself: an exalted fusion of the architect's elevated tone with the painter's gift for rich, meaningful gestures and theatrical settings and situations.

As always, even after a decade on the job,

Mancinelli is taken aback whenever he confronts the three altarpieces in this room. When he finds words, he says: "The funny thing with Raphael is that, if you didn't know these three paintings were by the same painter, you would think they were by three different painters. Each one represents the high point of a different phase for him."

Raphael's *Transfiguration* figured in an experiment in reproduction that began in 1977, when Vatican Museums administrator Persegati read of an exhibition at the Boston Museum of Fine Arts displaying the results of large-format Polaroid photography of a fifteenth-century tapestry, *The Martyrdom of St. Paul*. Using a camera that can produce forty-by-eighty-inch and twenty-by-twenty-four-inch prints in one minute, Polaroid Studios in Cambridge, Massachusetts, and the Boston Museum had collaborated on one-to-one reproduction as a tool that could enable art historians and conservators to examine an extremely high-quality photograph of a work of art in a matter of minutes.

Persegati commissioned such a photographic study of the *Transfiguration*, which had been restored under Mancinelli's direction between 1972 and 1976. The principal problems had been caused by the painting's stay in Paris from 1797 to 1816 as one of Napoleon's prisoners of war. After cleaning it, the Louvre technicians varnished it with a yellow pigment that eventually turned its predominantly blue tones to green. Worse still, they reinforced its old wooden support with a metal framework that, instead of conserving the painting, caused new damages when cracks in the wooden support were not permitted to expand freely. This problem was solved in the 1970s by replacing the French addition with a new wooden framework which not only allows the panel's wood to expand and contract freely, but also

prevents it from warping. A specially designed metal structure now supports the panel and sustains the individual elements of the wooden framework. Previous damages were corrected and the offending varnish was removed, along with some old stucco that covered the colors in many places. Underneath, fortunately, the original colors were intact.

Early in 1979, Polaroid dispatched a team of photographers and technicians to the Vatican. Since the *Transfiguration* is fifteen feet high by nine feet wide, the giant camera had to be placed on a hydraulic platform to permit the photographers to reproduce details from all areas of the painting. A huge darkroom had to be built for the camera inside the museum. Photographing the sixteen different exposures needed for one-to-one reproduction of the painting required pulleys, sandbags and scaffolding to support the camera. Another thirteen shots magnified postcard-size sections of the painting to twenty-by-twenty-four-inch format.

In 1980, the Polaroid team's results were shown at Harvard University's Fogg Art Museum in an exhibition called "A Masterpiece Close-Up: The *Transfiguration* by Raphael." Vatican Museums Director-General Carlo Pietrangeli says this "absolutely perfect reproduction of a masterpiece" makes "complex paintings like the *Transfiguration*—hitherto inaccessible because of location or inadequate lighting—available for in-depth study by everyone." And, adds curator Mancinelli, "It gives me a chance to show scholars and the public things they don't see at four yards' distance. Our restoration established that the painting was unfinished, but now, with the help of these reproductions and blow-ups, I can prove it easily. Look at this enlargement of the foot of the Prophet Elijah. The toes and

Raphael, predella panels from *The Coronation of the
Virgin* altarpiece, 1502–03. OPPOSITE ABOVE *The Annun-
ciation*. OPPOSITE BELOW *The Adoration of the Magi*.
ABOVE *The Presentation in the Temple*.

part of the foot are just sketched. The face of the first deacon is finished; the face of the second deacon is sketched."

The Polaroid invention uses one lens and a piece of light-sensitive film to transfer an image from negative to positive, thereby avoiding the grainy, diffuse look of a blow-up, which is merely an enlargement of a miniature negative. The compression of all chemical processing into a single step performed on the spot enables the photographer to compare his picture with the original immediately and to make necessary improvements in lighting or color balance for a retake. Mancinelli, however, differs with Pietrangeli as to the method's absolute perfection. "There are just too many colors for one camera, but the result is probably nearer perfection than any other form of reproduction. Certainly, as an instrument of research, this camera is quite perfect. Photography is sharper than the human eye, and now you are able to concentrate on the smallest detail."

In the showcases on the other walls of the Raphael Room are tapestries designed by Raphael showing ten scenes from the Acts of the Apostles, including *The Stoning of St. Stephen* and *The Conversion of Saul*. (His cartoons for the project are in London's Victoria and Albert Museum.) Commissioned by Pope Leo X in 1515 to decorate the side walls of the Sistine Chapel's presbytery and executed by Pieter van Aelst of Brussels, they were stolen by soldiers of Charles V of Spain during the sack of Rome in 1527. The soldiers burned the lower halves of some of the tapestries in an effort to extract the gold threads. Recovered a quarter of a century later, the tapestries were exhibited in the Gallery of Tapestries for three centuries and then transferred to the new Pinacoteca. "You can see the damage that was done by the soldiers," says Mancinelli, pointing to

jagged cuts across the bottom of *The Blinding of Elima*. "They must have stopped when they discovered that the thread was mostly silver just tinted with real gold and decided they could get more money for it as a tapestry."

Leaving the Raphael Room, you may still find yourself transfixed. If so, one way to refocus the eyes is, upon entering the ninth room, to take one last look back through the door at the *Transfiguration*'s swirl of light and movement, then glance at the guard's black-and-white closed-circuit television set monitoring the attitudes and activities of *Transfiguration* viewers.

In the next small room, Mancinelli introduces us to another victim of vandalism: a golden *St. Jerome in the Wilderness* painted by Leonardo da Vinci in 1480. This atmospheric tempera-on-wood vision of the ascetic hermit amidst dark, craggy rocks was once owned by the Swiss portrait painter Angelica Kauffmann (1741–1807), who died in Rome. A few years thereafter, Napoleon's uncle, Cardinal Joseph Fesch, was browsing in a Roman antique shop when he discovered that the torn-off torso of St. Jerome was being used as the lid of a trunk. The cardinal, being a collector, recognized it as a Leonardo and set about tracking down the missing pieces. He found the saint's head serving as the seat of a stool at a shoemaker's. From the cardinal's scavenger hunt, five fragments were put together to restore the lost Leonardo completely. While its scars are visible, they are not gaping, but shimmer like reflections beneath the thick unbreakable glass.

Opposite the Leonardo is a tempera-on-wood Bellini *Pietà* that once crowned a large

OPPOSITE Raphael, *Faith*, *Hope* and *Charity*, panels from the *Baglioni Predella*, 1507.

ABOVE Raphael, *Transfiguration of Christ*, 1517–20, panel.
OPPOSITE Titian, *Madonna in Glory with Six Saints*, 1528, panel, transferred to canvas.

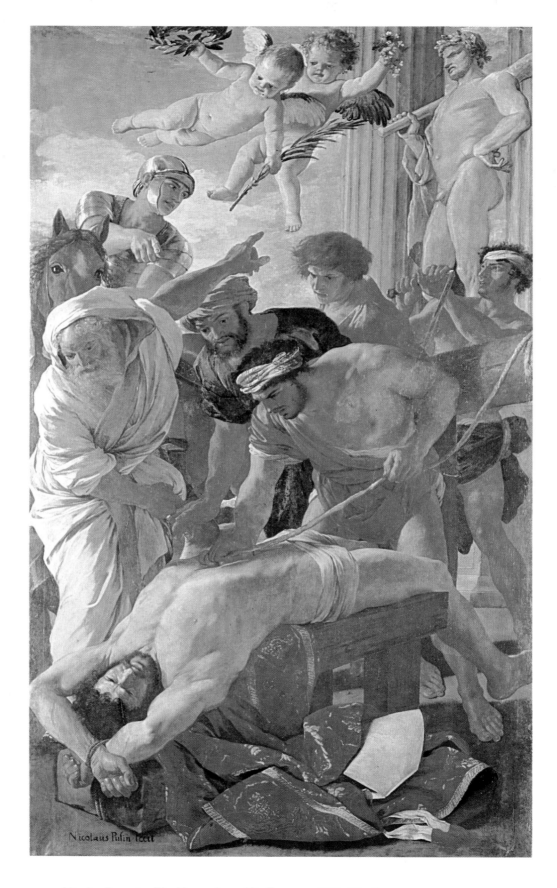

ABOVE Nicolas Poussin, *The Martyrdom of St. Erasmus*, 1628–29, oil on canvas.
OPPOSITE ABOVE Guercino, *The Incredulity of St. Thomas*, oil on canvas.
OPPOSITE BELOW Veronese, *St. Helena*, ca. 1580, oil on canvas.

Caravaggio, *The Deposition of Christ*, ca. 1603–04, oil on canvas.

TOP LEFT Giuseppe Maria Crespi, *Holy Family*, ca. 1735–40, oil on canvas.

TOP RIGHT Giuseppe Maria Crespi, *Prospero Lambertini (Pope Benedict XIV)*, 1740, oil on canvas.

ABOVE *Scenes from the Passion of Christ: Entry into Jerusalem, Last Supper, Kiss of Judas,* tapestry from a Tournai workshop, fifteenth century.

Visitors who resist the elevators can climb a spiral stair-case up to the Pinacoteca. It was built in 1932 by Giuseppe Momo. The balustrade, a chronology in bronze of papal history, was designed by Antonio Maraini.

Coronation of the Virgin altarpiece in Pesaro. Framed as a picture, it holds its own in distinguished company. It has been dated to about 1473 and marks a major turning point in the artist's growing mastery of atmospheric perspective. Its subtle graduations of light and color give it a spatial dimension almost beyond the limits of painting.

In the tenth room is Titian's *Madonna in Glory with Six Saints*—and therein lies yet another tale of mutilation. Painted in 1528 for a church in Venice, the picture came to Rome in 1770 and was purchased by Pope Clement XIV. Its top was originally semicircular, but in Rome it was cut down so that it could be hung alongside Raphael's *Transfiguration*. The now missing source of the rays above the Madonna and angels was the Holy Ghost, in the usual form of a dove. Opposite the Titian is an eloquent and dramatic *Coronation of the Virgin*, a Raphael commission that his pupils Giulio Romano and Giovan Francesco Penni executed from their master's designs five years after his death.

Two slightly uncharacteristic works of Paolo Veronese (1520–88) also adorn this room. Both belonged to the Sacchetti family. One is an allegorical scene that, along with two others now in Rome's Capitoline Gallery, formed a ceiling. The other is his *St. Helena*, a direct forerunner of the distinctly secular women who people Veronese's later banquets. In both paintings, one can perceive Veronese's juxtaposition of complementary colors to achieve brilliant luminosity.

Dominating the next room are four large works by Federico Fiori (1528–1612), better known as Barocci, a painter from Urbino whose mature works foreshadowed the seventeenth-century Baroque style. His *Rest on the Flight into Egypt*, also known as the *Madonna of the Cherries*, was commissioned in 1573 by Simonetto Anastagi of Perugia, who donated it to the Church of the Jesuits there. Two centuries later, when Pope Clement XIV suppressed the Jesuit order, the painting was brought to Rome's Quirinal Palace, and in the early nineteenth century, it was transferred to the Vatican. Two other Baroccis, the *Annunciation* and *Head of the Madonna*, are also quite representative, but another, the *Blessed Michelina*, with its wild and whirling sky, is classified as pre-Romantic in style and content.

In this Barocci room, Giorgio Vasari (1511–74), better known today as a biographer of artists than as a painter, is represented by a solemn, almost posed *Stoning of St. Stephen* that suffers from proximity to the next wall's vivid *Resurrection of Lazarus* by Girolamo Muziano (1528–92). The aging Michelangelo's praise for this work made the young Muziano famous.

The Pinacoteca's octagonal twelfth room offers a sparkling view of the Vatican Gardens and the dome of St. Peter's. You will need to gulp all the light and air that you can, for the room's strong points are brutal and magnificent. Start with Caravaggio's vehemently drawn, vigorous *Deposition of Christ*, in which the realistic faces and hands of all the characters except the crucified Christ seem to implore, even demand, our attention. The bearded and lined face of Nicodemus in the foreground is said to be a self-portrait of the artist. Mancinelli notes in passing that both Rubens and Cézanne painted versions of this *Deposition*. Next to it is Guido Reni's grim and gruesome oil-on-canvas *Crucifixion of St. Peter*, treated with the most effective kind of realism that condemns a vile deed by just portraying it.

Diagonally opposite the Caravaggio is one of Poussin's largest paintings, his flamboyant *Martyrdom of St. Erasmus* (1628–29).

Chained to a rack, the martyr is being disemboweled against a heroic stage backdrop of cherubs, columns and a statue of Hercules. Poussin's epic work was commissioned by Cardinal Francesco Barberini for the left tribune of St. Peter's, where it was long ago replaced by an eighteenth-century mosaic copy. It was already part of the Vatican Museums' picture collection in 1797, when Pius VI was forced to sign the humiliating Treaty of Tolentino with Napoleon, under which many of the Vatican's art treasures, including this one, were taken off to Paris. The French troops proceeded slowly and carefully with their precious acquisitions on an overland journey that lasted a year. The Poussin was displayed in the Louvre until 1816, when, in accord with the dictates of the Congress of Vienna, most of the works of art were given back to the Vatican. But the return trip was taken in haste, for Director-General Antonio Canova feared that the victorious allies might change their minds. Though made in winter, this journey took only three months, and Mancinelli deduces that "since you could draw one straight line connecting all the damages, they probably all happened on that return trip."

The damage included two holes, a gash across the face of the suffering saint, discoloration of the lusty brute who is torturing him and a loosening of the canvas that was threatening to shift the paint or flake it off like a peeling sunburn. To make matters worse, the aging of old glue and yellowing of old varnish were making

ABOVE *The Prophet Moses*, ca. 1120–30, fresco fragment.
LEFT Giorgio Vasari, *The Stoning of St. Stephen*, panel.

Poussin's whites yellow and his blues greenish. Before this treasure could be considered for transatlantic travel, Mancinelli and his curator colleagues all agreed that major surgery was mandatory.

Over a four-month restoration by Biagio Cascone in 1980, the holes were filled in with stucco, glues and varnishes were removed chemically, the painting was relined and restretched onto a flexible new frame and Poussin's work was given a thorough cleaning and retouching. The stuccoed holes were painted over with the vertical strokes of "integral restoration."

The next two rooms are loosely labeled "Seventeenth and Eighteenth Century." The first of them houses a harmonious assortment of religious pictures, including a pair of eloquent Pietro da Cortonas, *The Ecstasy of St. Theresa* and *The Virgin Appears to St. Francis*, and a strolling *St. Francis Xavier* painted by Anthony Van Dyck during his 1622–23 stay in Rome. When the Van Dyck first entered the Vatican collection in 1938, it was listed as the work of an anonymous painter. But art historians recognized its style, especially in the saint's ethereal hands, and documentary evidence and laboratory analysis later helped confirm it as a work Van Dyck created for the saint's altar in the Church of Il Gesù. The Flemish visitor to Rome, then in his early twenties, was still under the influence of Rubens, as his cherubs indicate. Rubens himself is represented in the second room by a fleshy, but not unduly bloody, *Apotheosis of Francis Gonzaga*, otherwise known as the *Triumph of Mars*. Though much of it is the work of pupils using Rubens's sketches, the exuberance of the figures and the harmony of the colors are clearly the master's own.

This fourteenth room is perhaps the least predictable in the Pinacoteca. Below the Rubens hang some uncannily telescopic,

Pietro da Cortona, *The Ecstasy of St. Theresa*, oil on canvas.

ABOVE Guercino, *Mary Magdalene*, 1623, oil on canvas.
RIGHT Sir Thomas Lawrence, *Portrait of King George IV*, 1816, oil on canvas.

almost photographic, astronomical observations painted by Donato Creti of Cremona (1671–1749) for an observatory in Rome. A series of eight small pictures (of the other planets then known—Mercury, Venus, Mars, Jupiter and Saturn—plus a comet, the sun and the moon), they seem to have been influenced by the recently condemned discoveries of Galileo (1564–1642).

Next to the Rubens is another Poussin that was restored in 1980, *The Battle of Gideon Against the Midianites*. A tiny fraction of the size of his *Erasmus*, this one wasn't in urgent need of restoration, Mancinelli admits: "Or so we thought. *The Battle of Gideon* being a night scene, we didn't realize how much the painting glowed until the restoration was done. All kinds of new elements have come out that will be studied for years. This was truly a metamorphosis!" Among these "new elements," Mancinelli cites Poussin's yellows, which had been thought to be the product of aging varnish, but can now be perceived as the artist's own tones. And the whole *Gideon* project paid a dividend when ultraviolet examination disclosed the inscription "Sacchetti" on the back of the canvas. While documentation indicated that the wealthy Sacchetti family had commissioned Poussin to paint *The Battle of Gideon* shortly after the young Frenchman arrived in Rome, this was confirmation in the artist's own scrawl.

The last room of the Pinacoteca is called the Portrait Gallery and it cuts across centuries to include Titian's 1542 posthumous portrait of the Venetian *Doge Niccolò Marcello*, a 1669 portrait of *Pope Clement IX* by Carlo Maratta (1625–1713), whose use of color in this gem of insight and intensity has been compared to that of the great masters from the Venetians to Velázquez, and a codgerly *Voltaire*, wearing nightcap and fur-trimmed robe, by Jean Hubert (1721–86), a French painter so noted for his series of portraits of the philosopher that he was nicknamed "Hubert-Voltaire." (Hubert also is described in the Vatican archives as "the inventor of a new genre, the silhouette: cutouts in black paper against a white background," though the name comes from Etienne de Silhouette, French controller general in 1757, whose stringent economies linked his name with this inexpensive art form.) There is also a portrait of *King George IV* of England, painted by Sir Thomas Lawrence in 1816. But we linger before a portrait by Giuseppe Maria Crespi (1665–1747) of *Prospero Lambertini* while he was still a cardinal and archbishop of Bologna. When Lambertini became Pope Benedict XIV in 1740, Crespi added the papal tiara and painted white vestments over his subject's scarlet cardinal's robes, which still shimmer through His Holiness's outer wear.

After pointing out the cardinal's new clothes, Mancinelli remarks: "Numerically, what you've seen here in the Pinacoteca is a little less than half of my painting collection; the rest is stored in our depots, where scholars can visit them. But, if you take into account the quality, most of what are in storage are second or third choices, though there are a few masterpieces which are in such bad shape that they would be hard to display and protect. Or there are space problems that prevent us from doing justice to a whole body of work." He points to a pink-cheeked dandy with ruffled sleeves and collar, posing at a palette but looking as though he would never smudge a pinkie with paint. "For instance, *him*," says Mancinelli. "All we have on display is this self-portrait, but he was primarily a painter of animals."

Mancinelli is referring to Wenceslas Peter (1742–1829), an Austrian, many of whose nature paintings were acquired by the

Gianlorenzo Bernini, *Portrait of a Young Man*, ca. 1635, oil on canvas.

Vatican in the nineteenth century. Mancinelli is assembling them for a small exhibition in an anteroom of the Pinacoteca. Rummaging in the depots, he found one other Peter painting depicting humans: Adam and Eve. From this, Mancinelli deduced that the animals were intended to be the inhabitants of the Garden of Eden. Inside the Vatican, a curator exults when he discovers a religious theme in what looked like secular art.

GALLERIES OF THE CANDELABRA, TAPESTRIES AND MAPS

Recrossing the court of the Pinacoteca, we climb the Simonetti Stairway again to rejoin the route to the Sistine Chapel two flights up. Once we have entered the Gallery of the Candelabra, we are committed to going forward without retreat, for, early in his tenure as secretary-general, which began in 1971, Walter Persegati (who used to do émigré resettlement work for Catholic welfare organizations in Chicago and New York) decreed one-way pedestrian traffic to eliminate bottlenecks and reassure visitors who start to feel lost that at least they are going in the right direction.

The Gallery of the Candelabra used to be known as the "Gallery of Miscellanea" for the five hundred small and relatively minor sculptures (from the fourth century B.C. to the third century A.D.) displayed there. And, among statues of *Nike* (Winged Victory) wearing a head of Athena from another statue and a *Ganymede* that was the ornamental motif of a table leg, one is hard put to discern the six marble lamp stands from which the Gallery of the Candelabra takes it name. Used for burning oil, wax or resin in Rome in the second century A.D., they can usually be found under the arches of the gallery's second and third sections.

The Gallery of Tapestries follows. Its principal exhibits resemble the Raphael tapestries we viewed in the Pinacoteca and were executed in the sixteenth century in the Brussels workshop of Pieter van Aelst from cartoons made in Rome. But those were "Old School," designed by Raphael himself with help, while these are "New School," designed by his pupils after his death and first exhibited in 1531 in the Sistine Chapel. Illustrating episodes from the life of Jesus, they include a three-part *Slaughter of the Innocents*, each wall hanging of which is bigger and more brutal than Brueghel's masterpiece in Vienna's Museum of Art History.

In every traditional museum in the world,

there is a work of art that inspires guides to note "how the eyes follow you" as you move past it. Such an attraction is the *Resurrection of Christ* in the Gallery of Tapestries. The hands and feet as well as the eyes of Jesus do indeed follow you as you walk—and so does the marble slab on which he stands. Even more of a miracle transpires two tapestries thereafter when *Christ Appears to the Disciples at Emmaus:* the table at which he is breaking bread also seems to turn.

The long, vast, vaulted Gallery of Maps was built by Ottaviano Mascherino (1524–1606) for Gregory XIII, the sixteenth-century pope whose own astronomical observations from the Tower of the Winds (also built by Mascherino directly above the Gallery of Tapestries) led to the Gregorian calendar reform. From 1580 to 1583, its walls were painted with the principal ports of the Tyrrhenian Sea on one 394-foot-long wall and all the ports of the Adriatic on the other by the Dominican friar Ignazio Danti of Perugia (1536–86), who was also a cosmographer, astronomer, engineer and professor of mathematics in his half-century on earth: truly a Renaissance man! On the twenty-foot short walls, Danti painted vivid scenes of the Siege of Malta, the Battle of Lepanto and the islands of Elba and Tremiti at one end and the four chief ports of the period— Civitavecchia, Genoa, Venice and Ancona— at the other, as well as various possessions of ancient Rome and the Church.

The barrel vault above the Gallery of Maps looks like a frescoed stamp collection: eighty miracles, allegories and events from church history and saintly chronicles. Many of these episodes are connected with the regions on the nearest maps below. The ceiling was the work of a team of Mannerist artists under the supervision of Cesare Nebbia (1534–1614) and Girolamo Muziano, whose *Resurrection of Lazarus* (now in the Pinacoteca) won the admiration of Michelangelo.

Wandering amidst the blues and greens of Danti's maps and gazing up at the dazzling gilded stucco ceiling with its statuary lunging out at you can be a dizzying experience. When I remarked to curator Mancinelli that I felt as though I were tiptoeing through Italy along the tops of the Apennines, he responded that this was precisely the effect Ignazio Danti confessed to seeking in a letter shortly before his death. "What surpasses all wonderment," a contemporary of Gregory XIII declared at the time, was how the gallery had been "decorated throughout with stuccoes and gilding and various paintings of the topography of the whole of Italy, all divided into pictures of the different provinces, to a very accurate scale. This is perhaps the finest example of its kind to be seen today." The Gallery of Maps was the most important cartographical enterprise of the Renaissance.

Last of the four successive galleries is that of St. Pius V (1504–72). It contains seventeenth-century tapestries from Rome's Barberini workshops and a pair of sixteenth-century Flemish tapestries: a *Coronation of the Virgin* from cartoons by Raphael's "New School" and a formal 1525 *Religion, Justice and Charity* by Pieter van Aelst that once decorated the bottom of the throne of Pope Clement VII. Older and far more valuable, on the opposite wall, are two from Tournai, the most important Flemish tapestry center of the fifteenth century: *Episodes from the Passion* and *Tapestry of the Credo.* Both were gifts from Maria Cristina of Bourbon, Queen Regent of Spain, to Leo XIII toward the end of the last century.

At the end of the gallery is the uppermost of three chapels, built one above the other by the sainted Pius V, who rose to the papacy from the post of inquisitor-general and whose brief but severe reign (1566–72) put

Latin names of remote rivers, provinces and tribes of eastern Europe mark this panel in the Gallery of Maps.

Catholicism's Counter-Reformation on the political offensive; among other deeds, he deposed Queen Elizabeth I of England in 1570 (it had little effect on her) and wrote to console Mary Queen of Scots in captivity. This chapel of his is dedicated to St. Michael. Its dome is decorated with a fresco of *The Fall of Lucifer and the Rebel Angels* painted by Giorgio Vasari and Federico Zuccari in the sixteenth century. Frescoes

below it were added in the nineteenth century.

TOWER OF INNOCENT III

Fra Angelico is represented in the third room of the Pinacoteca, but we will see him at his best by walking over to the Tower of Innocent III, in the oldest part of the Apostolic Palace. We enter the tower through the Room of the Chiaroscuri, whose ceiling was designed by Raphael for Leo X but painted by his assistants, with further decorations added in 1582 by Giovanni Alberti and Ignazio Danti, the genius who painted the Gallery of Maps. In the center of the room stands a copy of the wooden model made by Michelangelo sometime between 1558 and 1561 for the dome of St. Peter's, embellished by the architects who completed Michelangelo's mission more than a quarter of a century later, Giacomo della Porta and Domenico Fontana.

One room beyond is the private chapel which Nicholas V in 1447 commissioned Fra Angelico to decorate with frescoes. Fra Angelico (the Dominican friar Giovanni da Fiesole, who lived from 1400 to 1455) worked for four years on two series of paintings for the chapel, which is sometimes called Fra Angelico's instead of Nicholas V's. On its upper walls are *Stories of St. Stephen;* on the lower walls are *Stories of St. Lawrence.* They are considered masterpieces of the artist's maturity, blending the brilliance of the Renaissance with the mystical fervor of medieval painters. Beneath the starry ceiling and cobalt skies that are uniquely Fra Angelico's, the two saints are ordained, preach, give alms, are judged and martyred with a quiet serenity that serves only to heighten the artist's and our compassion for the poor, blind and bereaved to whom they minister. As Director-General Pietrangeli's predecessor, the Portuguese art historian Deocletio Redig de Campos, has written:

> Giovanni da Fiesole was a monk, and his painting was that of a monk. His was a true vocation, and this power of faith, this full conviction, comprises the very heart of his figures and breathes through his landscapes. Without the silence of the cloister, it would not be possible to account for his art, which treats life with that same temperate prudence with which the religious are taught by their monastic rules to treat the things of this world.

And yet, de Campos notes:

> In the aristocratic and idealizing art of the Italian Renaissance, only Angelico knew how to tell of the misery and suffering of the poor and infirm with such convincing truth and, at the same time, with such brotherly compassion.

If we return now to the Chapel of Pius V, we can turn to the left into the Sobieski Room and look at the largest painting in the Vatican, *Sobieski Liberates Vienna*, an epic oil on canvas, fifteen feet high by thirty feet wide, depicting the triumph of King John III Sobieski of Poland over the Turks just outside Vienna in 1683. Filled with horses, flags and groveling, vanquished Turks and illuminated by a rainbow over the easternmost Alps of Leopoldsberg and Kahlenberg, it is the masterpiece of the Polish painter Jan Matejko (1838–93), who renounced payment of his 80,000-florin fee (from a group of Polish noblemen) provided his painting be presented to Pope Leo XIII on the bicentenary of the liberation of Vienna. Back in the Gallery of the Candelabra, that presentation ceremony is portrayed in a ceiling fresco.

Proceed through the Borgia Tower's Room of the Immaculate Conception, so named for its nineteenth-century frescoes by Francesco Podesti and its books and manuscripts all paying tribute to the Papal Bull of December 8, 1854, in which Pius IX proclaimed the dogma of Immaculate Conception. The edict itself, in many languages, is in an elaborate golden showcase, made in Paris, that is the centerpiece of the room. Now you stand at the doors of the Raphael Rooms *(Stanze di Raffaello)*, waiting to confront some of the greatest art in the Vatican Museums.

Dr. Fabrizio Mancinelli, curator of Byzantine, medieval and modern art.

THE RAPHAEL ROOMS

E OWE THE Raphael Rooms to Pope Julius II, who didn't want to sleep in the Borgia Apartment directly below because he had many "bad and wicked memories" of his Borgia predecessor, Alexander VI. Instead, he commissioned Raphael to decorate four rooms for him on the second floor of the Apostolic Palace. Raphael began the work in 1508 and it was completed in 1524 by his assistants. Raphael died in 1520, so he never saw the rooms as we see them today.

Only the second room, the Room of the Segnatura, so called because papal documents were sealed there, is almost entirely by Raphael. The theme of this room is the glorification of divinely inspired human intellect. The *Disputa* (Disputation Concerning the Holy Sacrament) on the west wall was probably the first fresco to be painted. It represents theology and shows theologians of all eras, including St. Jerome and St. Gregory on the left and Pope Sixtus IV and Dante on the right, gathered around an altar on which is displayed the Host, the spiritual focus of the picture, unifying the earthly realm and the heavenly realm, where God the Father, Christ, the Virgin and St. John the Baptist are enthroned among New Testament saints and Old Testament prophets and patriarchs.

Dante appears again in *Parnassus*, a tribute to the arts, along with Virgil, Sappho, Boccaccio and the blind Homer, to whom the artist has given the features of the *Laocoön* sculpture in the Octagonal Court.

The fresco on the east wall, *The School of Athens*, is dedicated to philosophy, and its two central figures, shown strolling through a grand basilica designed by Bramante, are the white-bearded Plato (to whom Raphael has given the features of Leonardo da Vinci) and Aristotle, the greatest philosophers of antiquity. Socrates is at the left, ticking off points on his fingers, and below him, Pythagoras demonstrates his theories on a

OPPOSITE Raphael's fresco *The School of Athens* dominates the Room of the Segnatura. The dado below was painted by Perin del Vaga after the original wooden paneling was destroyed during the Sack of Rome in 1527. Among the designs in the inlaid marble floor are the crossed keys of Pope Nicholas V.

slate. On the right, Ptolemy contemplates a celestial globe and Euclid bends down to draw a circle on another slate. The ragged old man sprawled on the steps is Diogenes. The white-robed Raphael himself looks out at us on the left, and the brooding Heraclitus leaning his head on his hands is a portrait of Michelangelo; Raphael changed his original composition to pay this tribute to his lonely rival.

The Room of Heliodorus was the second to be painted and, although it was designed by Raphael, not all of the work was done by him. Still, it contains one of his masterpieces, the *Mass at Bolsena*, which shows a famous miracle that took place in the thirteenth century. A Bohemian priest who did not believe in the transubstantiation of the bread and wine into the body and blood of Christ was celebrating Mass when the consecrated Host shed drops of blood in the form of a cross on the altar cloth. Julius was particularly devoted to this miracle, and Raphael has included him and two of his cardinals on the right.

Julius appears again in the *Expulsion of Heliodorus*, which gave this room its name. We see him at left, being borne in on a litter and watching attentively as the would-be temple robber is driven away by a heavenly horseman and two angelic warriors in answer to the prayer of the high priest.

Over the window opening toward the Belvedere and the Vatican Gardens is the third of the miracles that are the theme of this room, which is devoted to divine intervention in human affairs. The *Liberation of St. Peter* shows an angel delivering the saint from Herod's prison so that he can obey the injunction to preach the gospel all over the world.

The Room of Heliodorus is completed by the *Expulsion of Attila*, based on an event that took place in the fifth century, when

Pope Leo III, unarmed, routed the king of the Huns near Ravenna through the miraculous intervention of St. Peter and St. Paul. Raphael has transferred the event to the gates of Rome and given the pope the features of Leo X, who was elected after the death of Julius in 1513.

The Room of the Incendio, or fire, was painted from 1514 to 1517 and used by Leo as a music room. It was the last of the chambers to be decorated by Raphael, who did only the designs and some of the cartoons, leaving the execution to his pupils. The fresco that gives it its name is *Fire in the Borgo*, which is based on an event that was believed to have taken place in the year A.D. 847. Pope Leo IV, it was said, had extinguished with the sign of the cross a blaze raging through the Borgo Santo Spirito, the still-picturesque borough between the Vatican and Castel Sant' Angelo.

In the fourth room, some of the works may be based on Raphael's designs, but most of them were painted by Giulio Romano and Giovan Francesco Penni after their master's death in 1520. It is called the Hall of Constantine, for its subject is the life of the Roman emperor who legalized and later embraced Christianity in the fourth century. Although the *Battle of the Milvian Bridge*— where in the year 312 Constantine defeated Maxentius, his rival for control of the empire —is by Giulio Romano, a few sketches for it by Raphael do exist.

In the room of the Incendio a few years ago, salts started oozing out of a fresco over a window facing onto the Belvedere Court, which is now a congested, polluted parking lot and thoroughfare in downtown Vatican City. The fresco was *The Oath of Leo III*, painted by Raphael's assistants; its subject (who reigned from 795 to 816) had the features of the then-reigning Leo X.

The Vatican Museums' scientific

Fire in the Borgo gives the Room of the Incendio its name. Raphael designed this room, but the painting was executed by his pupils, Giulio Romano and Giovan Francesco Penni.

laboratories were faced with the crucial problem of determining the origin of the salts and how to cope with them. They resulted from a chain of chemical reactions between the mortar in the wall and pollutants in the air: sulfur dioxide from burning coal, nitrous oxides from auto exhausts and hydrogen chloride, which escapes from smokestacks of incinerators burning garbage, particularly plastics.

These pollutants dissolve in rainwater and water vapor to form acids: sulfurous acid, nitric acid and hydrochloric acid. These, in turn, react with the components of mortar, particularly calcium carbonate, to create chemical compounds that cause crumbling

ABOVE The Room of Heliodorus is devoted to the theme
of divine intervention in human affairs. On the window
wall is the *Mass at Bolsena*. At left, the *Expulsion of
Heliodorus*. BELOW *Parnassus*, in the Room of the Segnatura.

Original Sin is one of fifty-two biblical scenes decorating the vaults of Raphael's Loggia, which is sometimes called "Raphael's Bible."

and porosity even in the Raphael Rooms' five-foot-thick walls. These compounds are called *saltpeter* by restorers, but the term covers a multitude of salts: calcium sulfite and calcium sulfate, calcium chloride and potassium nitrate, of which the last (KNO_3) is the true saltpeter, against which there are hardly any chemical reagents that could have been used.

Fortunately, tests showed that the offending ooze consisted largely of the first and third compounds, both of which are soluble in water, with only a tiny trace of potassium nitrate. And, thanks to research done after the Florence flood of 1966, there were prescribed chemical methods of coping with these salts.

For example, calcium sulfite (and, for that matter, calcium sulfate, which, hydrated, is gypsum) can be combined with ammonium carbonate to re-form much of the calcium carbonate that was the main ingredient of the mortar. The ammonium sulfate that is also formed by this reaction can be combined with barium hydroxide to form barium sulfate, which is insoluble and which forms fine crystals that plug the pores left by the previously destroyed calcium carbonate. And, while ammonium hydroxide is formed, too, it is a highly soluble gas that can be dispersed gradually into the air.

"From there on," says chief scientist Nazzareno Gabrielli, making it sound easy, "all we had to do was bore in several large cavities, a little more than a yard deep, into the outside wall and place little heaters inside to pump hot air forward, for three or four dry months. Using a method developed by a professor in Florence, we kept applying to the fresco little tissue papers soaked in the fluids we'd prescribed. Whenever the tissues got dirty from the salts, we'd apply new dabs of tissue and, with this treatment from both ends, the salts were rendered insoluble."

What little true saltpeter had formed was removed by continuous washing and absorbent dabbing as well as heat and humidity treatments. This is possible because the true saltpeter is highly soluble: while it can't be changed chemically, it is absorbed through water and therefore susceptible to such physical measures as soaking and dabbing.

"We now have the means," Gabrielli continues, "to combat whatever salts are formed when a bird builds a nest in the same wall as a fresco or a toilet starts seeping organic matter through." But his big hurdle, he admits, was to convince the restoration conference that he ought to try these relatively new post–Florentine flood techniques in so ancient and precious a place as the Raphael Rooms. "It took almost a year before we could start," he says, "but eventually everybody was convinced that the danger of doing nothing was at least as great as the need to do something."

On the other hand, the door from the fourth Raphael Room, the Hall of Constantine, to Raphael's Loggia has been either partly or fully closed to the public since 1975, when a restoration was undertaken and something went wrong. An arcade with forty-eight Old Testament and four New Testament scenes overhead, four to an archway, this enchanted corridor is sometimes called "Raphael's Bible." Though windowed-in many years ago, the Loggia had for three centuries been open to the weather, protected only by pillars from wind, rain and dirt. So quickly had the Loggia deteriorated that Giovanni da Udine (1487–1564), who stuccoed the walls and pillars with Raphael's original team, had to give them major restoration less than fifty years later. And rehabilitation of its fifty-two ceiling frescoes —designed by Raphael and executed by his assistants Giulio Romano and Giovan

Francesco Penni, Perin del Vaga and others between 1517 and 1519—was long overdue by the middle of the last decade.

The hand of man—from Garibaldi's soldiers peeling off parts of one wall to tourists carving their initials into the woodwork—had wrought further ravages requiring repairs. But what went wrong in the middle of the 1970s centers on a new solvent, developed in the Vatican laboratories, that was used on the first six of the Loggia's fifty-two frescoes. In the first arch—housing *God Divides the Light from the Dark, God Divides the Land from the Water, God Creates the Sun and the Moon* and *God Creates the Animals*—it worked perfectly. On the first two frescoes of the second bay, however—the *Creation of Eve* and *Original Sin*, in which the serpent has a human head—a film formed and the restoration was stopped. About a year later a cure was found, but, as curator Mancinelli put it: "What was damaged cannot be undamaged. We have retouched it, in a recognizable way, with vertical strokes that, from up close, you can recognize were not made in Raphael's time, but which don't mar the general appearance from viewing distance."

Despite this near-disaster, it is to be hoped that Raphael's Loggia will be reopened by the time you read this, for even in its present form, it is a festive delight: pious yet playful up above, while in the stuccowork on walls and pillars, one perceives elephants, flowers, statues, myths, portraits of Raphael at work and Michelangelo wearing a felt hat, a bishop kneeling to receive Pope Leo X's blessing as His Holiness passes through this Loggia and reliefs reproducing sculptures that include Donatello's *St. George* and the *Apollo Belvedere*.

There is even a relief of a plasterer with trowel and pan, who is presumed to be Giovanni da Udine, to whose stuccowork the most credit for the Loggia's gaiety must go. This type of decoration was named "grotesque" after the grottoes in which men of the Renaissance were discovering ancient Roman stuccoes. Although artists had been experimenting with grotesque decoration since the late fifteenth century, it was Giovanni da Udine who rediscovered the original Roman mixture of lime, plaster and marble sawdust. Grotesque (the name persists today in more sinister context) reached its apex of expression as an art form in Raphael's Loggia.

Raphael's Loggia was originally open to the weather but is now glassed in. The walls and pillars were stuccoed by Giovanni da Udine in a type of decoration known as "grotesque."

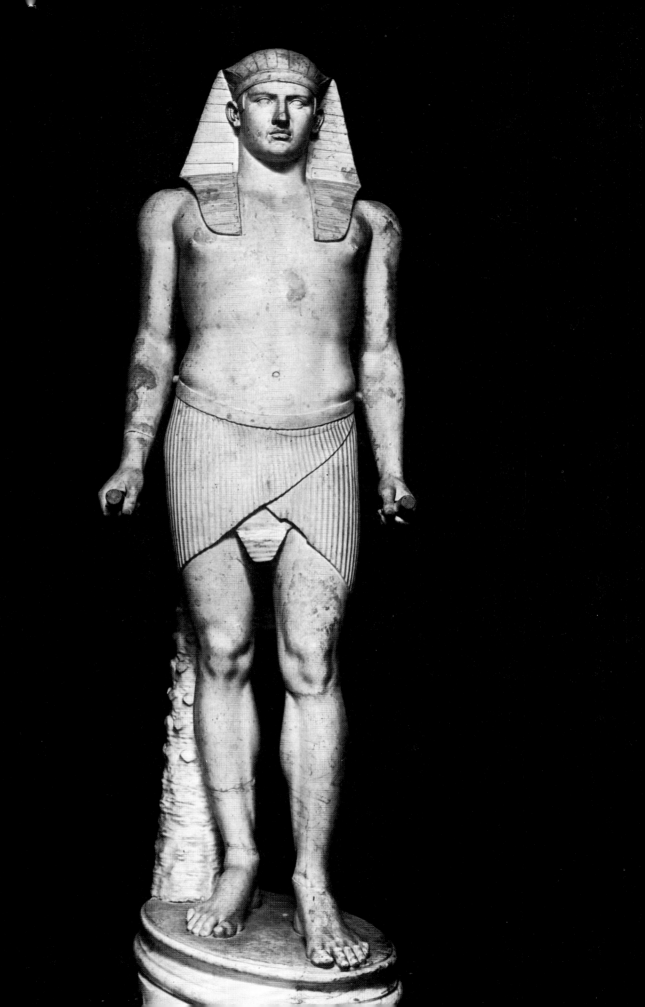

THE GREGORIAN EGYPTIAN MUSEUM

SOON AFTER THE FIRST NAPOLEONIC expedition to Egypt at the turn of the nineteenth century, Popes Pius VI and Pius VII received gifts of objects dating from the time of the pharaohs, but nobody then knew what to make of these mysterious trophies or their inscriptions. Then, in 1821, the French scholar Jean-François Champollion, using the Rosetta Stone discovered in Egypt in 1799, established the principles by which it was possible to decipher Egyptian hieroglyphics. The Egyptology boom that ensued in Europe led Pope Gregory XVI to found the world's first museum displaying Egyptian antiquities in installations that sought to re-create the world of the pharaohs.

The Gregorian Egyptian Museum was opened in 1839. While all who attended the inauguration marveled at the ten rooms of wonders wrought by Father L. M. Ungarelli, the father of Egyptology in Italy, little heed was paid thereafter to Ungarelli's stated concept of his museum's mission: to clarify, with its treasures, how people lived in the days of the Old Testament and to use that knowledge in widening our understanding of the past.

For more than a century after Ungarelli, the Vatican's Egyptian Museum functioned without its own chief; it was the headless torso of an infant science administered by the other curators. Thus, in 1966, when Monsignor Gianfranco Nolli, then a forty-seven-year-old Egyptologist and teacher of Holy Scriptures in Rome, joined the Vatican staff as the Egyptian Museum's first official full-time curator, he inherited what he describes as "a mess. Everything had been put into two rooms which had been closed to the public for years because who wants to look at a warehouse?" Relatively recent gifts from Egypt had been lumped together with ancient objects found in Italy that were copies or imitations of Egyptian objects.

Monsignor Nolli soon managed to regain the other eight rooms. But then he had to.

OPPOSITE *Antinoüs*, Hadrianic Period, A.D. 117–138, marble.

come to grips with nineteenth-century notions of how to re-create ancient Egypt. "Nobody, not even Ungarelli, had ever seen Egypt," Nolli says. "And so they invented a romantic Egypt"—an Egypt of starry-skied ceilings and a décor anticipating the excesses of Cecil B. De Mille.

Still, his museum having been a milestone in itself—the first in the history of Egyptology—Nolli felt obligated to pay brief homage within its walls to the romantic concept, but at the same time to "substitute exploration and insight for imagination and fantasy." So the first two rooms that one enters present what Nolli calls "a modern concept of ancient Egypt as it *is*."

One room is a ruin and the other a tomb. In the ruin—complete with holes in the wall from hammering by Vatican workmen and overhead clouds that are not painted but just bare ceiling—an inscription exhorts us in hieroglyphics: "Come and see the beautiful statues that Gregory has gathered together in this museum." This, says Nolli, was done for the inauguration and was probably the first time any inscription was ever translated from Italian *into* Egyptian.

Three steps down, and we are in an underground room of a tomb in the Valley of the Kings. The tomb room is a reproduction enlarged in proportion, but its six mummies, while assembled from various tombs and periods, are authentic. This may be why the tomb today is thronged with young people with sketch pads seeking to capture the undeniable, irrefutable posture of death. The

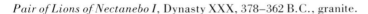

Pair of Lions of Nectanebo I, Dynasty XXX, 378–362 B.C., granite.

mummies are housed in double Plexiglas under constant temperatures and with indirect lighting. All six have been restored from time to time, but they probably won't need further restoration, says Nolli, for modern science and the Vatican laboratories have done so well at permanent preservation that other museums are sending their specialists over to study these techniques. Total disinfestation removes not just all living organisms, mostly worms, but their eggs, too. And, to arrest further deterioration of the bodies, natural oils are used that don't dissolve like chemical substances. "With a soap," says Nolli, "you want it to dissolve. But these natural substances, even with time, never change. Once the process of deterioration is arrested, it stops permanently, just the way a diamond is unchangeable forever."

A couple of mummies are displayed not just under Plexiglas, but in two halves of a modern contoured wooden coffin delicately painted with Egyptian motifs. "Yes, if you think about it, it is unreal," Nolli admits. "But I had two thoughts in mind. Of course, the first was that we want the public to see the entire mummy without endangering it. But the second was this: We want to remind you that you are seeing not just a work of art or a treasure of Egyptology, but a human body, which is, in a sense, sacred. The dead must command the respect of the living."

On that note, we ascend three steps into the two remaining rooms of romantic nineteenth-century Egyptology: a Cinecittà

version of a Middle Eastern landscape of painted perfect skies, floors of marble (which didn't exist in ancient Egypt) and, visible through a *trompe l'oeil* window, a fresco view of Nero's tomb. The exhibits in this third room are second- and third-century A.D. Roman sculptures inspired by Egyptian art and assembled by Gregory XVI from Hadrian's Villa at Tivoli and the Temple of Isis in the Campus Martius; hence it is sometimes called "The Room of the Imitations."

This room contains a large statue of *Antinoüs*. Seven foot two and hewn from Grecian marble that has stayed whiter-than-white, it has a remarkably contemporary look. Antinoüs was a youth of legendary beauty, the Bithynian-born (ca. A.D. 110) favorite slave and constant companion of the Roman Emperor Hadrian until, on a journey to Egypt in the year 130, he drowned in the Nile—while saving Hadrian's life, some say. Antinoüs was deified by the emperor and worshipped by his subjects. Hadrian founded the Egyptian city of Antinoöpolis in his honor and also had his birthplace in what is now Turkey renamed Antinoöpolis. A cult of Antinoüs was inaugurated, money was coined with his image on it and many busts and statues were carved in his memory.

Room five is what Nolli terms "neutral," for it is neither lushly romantic nor resolutely modern. But there is nothing else neutral about it. A sixteenth-century semicircular hall designed by Bramante, it makes a splendid gallery for giant statuary of remarkable grace and delicacy, including an inbred royal family trio of king, queen and sister.

"Whose sister?" I wondered. "The king's or the queen's?"

"It doesn't matter now," said Nolli, "and it didn't matter then. You see, the king and queen were brother and sister, so the sister-

BELOW *Double-faced Herm of Apis and Isis*, Hadrianic Period, A.D. 117–138, marble.
OPPOSITE *Torso of Nectanebo I*, Dynasty XXX, 378–362 B.C., granite. The back-pillar is inscribed.

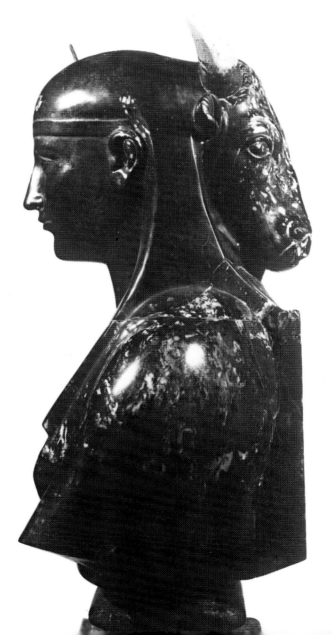

in-law was their sister, too." The king, it turns out, was Ptolemy II, in whose reign (285–246 B.C.) the Old Testament was translated from Hebrew into Greek.

"Not Egyptian?"

"No, from the fourth century before Christ to the seventh century after Christ, when the Muslims invaded, Greek was the language of Egypt. Oh, the people spoke in local dialect, but the official language of culture and commerce was Greek. And this translation of the Bible was one of the greatest cultural events of ancient times; there is nothing parallel to it."

At the center of Bramante's hemicycle stands a dark granite colossal statue of *Queen Tuya*, mother of Ramses the Great, dating from around 1300 B.C. There is also the throne of a lost statue of Ramses, who reigned for sixty-seven years (1292–1225 B.C.); it was he who built the great rock temple at Abu Simbel. Also in the hemicycle is the oldest representation of a pharaoh in the Egyptian Museum: the head of

Mentuhotep from a statue which has unfortunately been lost. Lost, too, is the record of which Mentuhotep he is; in the Eleventh Dynasty (2033–1890 B.C.), five pharaohs bore that name. Carved on the back of his neck are hieroglyphics identifying him as "the divine benefactor Mentuhotep," but the rest of the inscription has been mutilated.

The five remaining rooms are smaller and so are the artifacts on display: amulets and scarabs (one of them commemorating the excavation of an artificial lake sometime between 1405 and 1370 B.C.); statuettes; mummies of a cat, a sparrow hawk and a serpent; papyri; and the Carlo Grassi Collection of Egyptian minor antiquities, donated in 1951 to Pius XII by the Italian ambassador to Egypt and his wife. It consists of several hundred objects dating from the Coptic period of Christian art (which reached its height in the fifth and sixth centuries) through the Muslim conquest of Egypt (639–42) all the way to a duck-shaped thirteenth-

BELOW *Queen Tuya*, Dynasty XIX, ca. 1300 B.C., granite.

RIGHT *Mummy Case*, Dynasty XXIII, ca. 930–800 B.C., painted sycamore wood.

Stele of Queen Hatshepsut, Dynasty XVIII, 1449–1442 B.C., sandstone. The stele commemorates the queen's restoration of the walls around the necropolis of Thebes. She is shown here, dressed in the ceremonial regalia of a male pharaoh, offering gifts to the god Amun-Ra.

century pitcher. Because Egypt suggests images of great temples and powerful pharaohs, it is easy to forget the Egyptians' love of fantasy and humor until one confronts the small objects of art in the Grassi Collection and some of the rooms preceding it. (Aside from the Grassi Collection, the only other major post-Ungarelli acquisition of the Egyptian Museum has been fifteen pieces, including three wooden sarcophagi, given by a Turkish viceroy of Egypt in the late nineteenth century.) And, in one of those last rooms is *The Temple Bearer (Naophoros)*, a green basalt sculpture of a priest holding a small temple in his hands. What makes the statue precious is a long inscription covering the priest's robe and the sides of the temple. Describing the life of the priest during the first invasion of Egypt by the Persians in 525 B.C., it is virtually the only primary source of information about a little-known period of Egyptian history.

Beyond the Grassi Collection, but closed to the public, is the stunning Stairway of the Assyrian Reliefs: muted carvings beneath a busy Renaissance ceiling frescoed in a lush grotesque style of leaves, flowers, faces, angels and masks. Most of the fragments of

relief and the inscriptions in cuneiform (the writing of ancient Assyria, Babylon and Persia) come from the palaces of Sargon II (who reigned from 722 to 705 B.C.) and his son and successor, Sennacherib (705–681 B.C.), and celebrate the military exploits of the two kings. The inscriptions are lovely to look at just as abstract art, while the carvings themselves, once the eye adjusts from the glare of the vault, are exquisitely detailed down to the last toenail of the last soldier.

More than a decade ago, Nolli obtained permission from Pope Paul VI to create a Palestinian section for his museum. "In order to comprehend the total concept of Egyptology," he argued then, "one must understand what Egypt brought to Palestine." This, of course, would bring the Egyptian Museum back to its original concept as an amplification of life in Old Testament times. However, in Pope Paul's lifetime the Vatican hierarchy never gave the necessary orders to begin renovation, even though no extra space or acquisitions were involved. Nolli's plan entails merely consolidating the nine thousand objects (many of them fragments, but virtually all on display) and redesigning the original ten rooms into six or seven larger rooms. At last, in 1981 his long-approved renovation took a giant step toward realization when it was put into the work program for prompt completion, and the Gregorian Egyptian Museum was designated for renaming as the Vatican Museum of Oriental Antiquities, in which the Egyptian portion will be a major section.

OPPOSITE Monsignor Gianfranco Nolli, curator of the
Gregorian Egyptian Museum.
BELOW The Simonetti Stairway provides a dramatic
background for two Egyptian sphinxes and a colossal
bust of the Emperor Hadrian.

THE GREGORIAN ETRUSCAN MUSEUM

ÓTH THE SIMONETTI STAIRWAY and the Stairway of the Assyrian Reliefs lead up to the Gregorian Etruscan Museum, which the active Pope Gregory XVI opened in 1837, two years ahead of his Egyptian Museum. The Etruscan Museum was a result of the first intensive archeological excavations in Etruria, the area of Tuscany and Lazio that includes Florence and Rome and whose southern portion was then part of the Papal States. An Etruscan Museum was established in Florence (now part of the Museo Archeologico) to house the treasures unearthed in northern Etruria, and the pope established a museum in the Vatican for objects found in southern Etruria.

The Gregorian Etruscan Museum had a head start over any other because in 1820 one of Gregory's predecessors, Pius VII, had charged Cardinal Bartolomeo Pacca with promulgating a law that would regulate excavations in the Papal States, protect against plunder and guarantee the Church first right to buy, at a fair price, any finds unearthed in Vatican territory. Unlike many such laws, the Pacca Edict did not pay mere lip service to those ideals but showed its teeth from the start. All private collections within the Papal States had to be inventoried and catalogued, with one copy presented to the government so that, henceforth, any new acquisition would be spotted. No excavation could begin without government permission, and each application had to state not only where the dig would be and what the excavators hoped to find, but also how its location was situated with regard to other monuments or ruins that might be damaged. When a permit was granted, an official overseer was appointed as a watchdog to make a daily accounting to the state.

Only once was there papal participation in a dig and that took place in the 1830s, when the Vatican was getting ready to open the museum and needed more exhibits. An excavation near Vulci, an ancient Etruscan town north of Tarquinia near the Tyrrhenian Sea, was carried out in partnership with the

OPPOSITE *Mars of Todi*, ca. 400 B.C., bronze.

brothers Campanari, local excavators who knew the territory and took half of what was found. "A large part of our Greek vase collection comes from this excavation," says the current curator of the Etruscan Museum, Professor Francesco Roncalli. "Otherwise, any object found had to be presented first to the state for inspection and evaluation by a special papal commission of archeologists and artists who used to decide whether or not the state wanted to buy it. If so, they would assign a price to it, which was usually much lower than the finder wanted, but which he had to accept. Many landowners resented this because they wanted to make more money from what was in their earth, so it

Head of a Young Woman, possibly from a figure of a goddess in a pediment frieze, late fourth or early fifth century B.C., terracotta.

didn't help, no matter how religious they were, to be told it was priestly law, *legge pretina.* They called it *legge cretina* [idiotic law].

"Last but not least," Roncalli continues, "the state put money where its words were. There was a fund of ten thousand escudi, a considerable sum, which was renewed annually, for acquisition. Virtually all of the contents of the Etruscan Museum were bought by the state. And the Pacca Edict worked so well that, in 1870, when the Papal States ceased to exist, the government of Italy took over the law word for word."

Though the Etruscan era can roughly be defined as the first millennium before Christ, Roncalli's initial problems came from the early nineteenth century:

"I inherited a museum [some twenty thousand objects, eighty to ninety percent of them on display] that was fashioned to the archeological tastes of its time. This meant, for example, that everything was classified by elements—bronzes in one room, stone in another, terracotta in another—regardless of chronology. The visitor was told nothing about the objects, which is terrible; nor were any records kept of what was deemed worthless then and often thrown away.

"Now, in my Etruscan tombs, you'll find Attic vases—that is, pottery made in Athens or Corinth—for the wealthy Etruscans were great importers of the best from everywhere: amber from the north, gold from Phoenicia and pottery from Greece. So the nineteenth-century Etruscologists were confronted with both Greek vases and local products. Since Etruscology was a new profession, most of these scholars were more familiar with classical Greek mythology and heroes: they could decipher Greek inscriptions far better than Etruscan terracotta. Which is why, in museums around the world, you'll notice there are nicely illuminated rooms for Greek

Fibula, from the Regolini-Galassi Tomb, Cerveteri, ca. 650 B.C., gold.

vases and dreary, dingy rooms for Etruscan art.

"This is how ours became the dark science, veiled in a mystique of ignorance that turned into romance when English writers described the sinister Etruscan landscape of deep ravines and told you to whom you had to address yourself to see a certain tomb and, over in the corner, you'd find the colonel's daughter making a drawing of it. Meanwhile, the image of Greek culture was one of light, sun and knowledge. This I have tried to change here, for there is no reason for it today."

Even more troublesome, he adds, was the nineteenth-century attitude toward restoration:

"They were interested mostly in the storytelling parts and, having put them together, they would fill in the rest of the vase with black shards and fragments found in the same tomb without trying to look for the right fragments that were often right there, too. Instead, they simply forced together the shards they had in hand and then painted everything over. In the cleanings, this became clear. Sometimes, just going through the deposits [rooms down in the basement or under the roof where unclassified pieces are stored], I'd find the right fragments, and then it became imperative to undo the old restoration and replace the wrong piece with the right piece. But not to paint it over again. In our restoration, the cracks show." And

dynamic Etruscologist, archeologist, linguist and scientific purist who would later, as director-general of the Vatican Museums, have the *Apollo Belvedere* stripped of its artificial limbs. Nogara, to Roncalli's regret, threw out much of the Etruscan Museum's artificial atmosphere, including several wooden chairs that had been made to order with Etruscan decorative motifs, but his vigorous impact, combined with the Falcioni acquisition, served to put the Etruscan Museum back on the Vatican map. In the 1920s, when Pius XI appointed Nogara director-general, an archeologist named Filippo Magi succeeded him as curator of the Etruscan Museum, so Roncalli, who replaced Magi in 1967, is only the third curator in his museum's history. The bearded, leonine son of a diplomat, Roncalli, a count by title, is no

indeed they do—red clay veins or scars on glittering black pottery—but this is part of the warts-and-all philosophy of "archeological restoration" that pervades the Vatican Museums.

With the loss of the Papal States in 1870, aggressive acquisition policies ceased in virtually all of the Vatican Museums. In the Etruscan Museum, though, this period of stagnation lasted for only thirty years. Then, at the turn of the century, toward the end of the twenty-five-year reign of Leo XIII (1878–1903), there were two important developments: Pope Leo bought the Falcioni Collection of Etruscan and Roman artifacts from a wealthy family in Viterbo. And, immediately following this sudden investment of Vatican money in art, the pope appointed the first full-time director for the Etruscan Museum.

That director was Bartolomeo Nogara, the

ABOVE *Amphora of the Achilles Painter*, middle of the fifth century B.C.
BELOW *Protome of a Winged Horse*, from the roof of a temple in Cerveteri, beginning of the fifth century B.C., terracotta.

Professor Francesco Roncalli, curator of the Etruscan Egyptian Museum.

relation to Pope John XXIII (1881–1963), who was born Angelo Giuseppe Roncalli of peasant stock, though the curator's father and the future Holy Father formed a firm friendship in Bulgaria in the 1920s, when both were stationed in Sofia as diplomats: the former representing Italy and the latter, the Holy See. Angelo Roncalli was already pope when he learned that young Francesco Roncalli was studying Etruscan archeology. "Well," he remarked, "you must come and see me sometime. I have a very nice museum that will interest you."

In that "very nice museum," the Falcioni Collection that Leo XIII acquired in 1900 occupies a small turret with three windows affording a grand panoramic view of much of Rome and, almost directly below it, the Vatican tennis courts. "I have been in here many times at all hours," Roncalli remarks, "and I have never seen anyone playing tennis." Such is the air of mystery attached to the Etruscan Museum and the Egyptian Museum just below that one almost imagines Etruscans and Egyptians emerging from their tombs by night to play mixed doubles. The Falcioni exhibits—gold jewelry and small bronze relics, mostly tiny—do not distract from fantasy.

Pius XI, who reigned from 1922 to 1939, was, along with Leo XIII, the other great friend of the Etruscan Museum in this century. "Every pope since then," says Roncalli, "has been more interested in modern art." In 1935, the Benedetto Guglielmi Collection of painted pottery, bronzes and jewelry was donated to the pope. The Guglielmis owned land around Vulci and had been excavating there since the nineteenth century. After the family collection was divided among the heirs, one of them, Benedetto, offered his share to the Vatican on condition that the objects be exhibited in a special room and a catalogue be published as soon as possible. Since the Vatican's Guglielmi Collection represents a little less than half of the family's archeological holdings, Roncalli stays in touch with the other heirs. "But they want to sell, not donate," he reports, "and I wouldn't dare to make an offer, since we don't buy." He would guess that their asking price might be at least two million dollars.

Roncalli was more personally involved with his museum's third collection: ceramics donated by Mario Astarita to Paul VI in 1967. Descended from a banking family, Astarita started gathering pottery from excavations near Naples around the turn of the century. Later, he expanded into acquiring objects from other parts of Italy and buying up whole collections. Because he and his wife were childless, he began to worry that his relatives might divide the collection after his death and disperse it on the international antiquities market. Eager to keep the collection intact, he donated it to the Vatican Museums on the same conditions under which Guglielmi had given his collection, so he could see it exhibited and catalogued in his lifetime. The first volume, on Astarita's Italian and Etruscan vases, by Arthur Dale Trendall, was published in 1976; the second, by Dietrich von Bothmer, is on Attic ceramics; and there will be at least another two volumes following that. Although he was almost blind, Astarita visited the Etruscan Museum often until his death in late 1979.

Next door to the Astarita Room is a rotunda of Greek vases that come under Roncalli's jurisdiction "because many of them were found in Etruscan tombs." Two masterpieces of Attic art of the sixth century B.C. now in this room owe much to Roncalli. The most famous is a black amphora (large two-handled vase) showing two exquisitely detailed figures against a bare orange

background. Ajax and Achilles have laid down their arms for a round of *morra*, an ancient counting game played with the fingers on the order of one-potato-two-potato. One figure is betting three; the other, four. It is signed by the potter and painter Exekias, the last and greatest artist of the rigidly two-dimensional black-figure style, with pride in both his potting and painting expressed as if the vase were speaking: "Exekias painted and shaped me." But Roncalli must be credited with an assist twenty-five centuries later. The amphora's lid had long been listed as missing, but the curator located it not so long ago. Where? In the same collection—displayed upside down as a vase in itself!

The other Attic masterwork is a wine vase by a prolific artist known as the Painter of Amasis. Roncalli put the vase together from "pieces in the deposits." Not only did the genius from Amasis use lavish colors to expand the austere two-color techniques of his time, but he also, Roncalli reports, "smoothed the surface from inside to make it thinner and lighter, like an eggshell."

The Etruscan Museum also has a small collection of Roman antiquities that were once mixed in with the Etruscan material but have now been given three rooms of their own between the Falcioni Collection and the Room of the Terra Cottas. The art and artifacts shown in the Antiquarium Romanum date from the second century B.C. to the fourth century A.D. and include reliefs showing three of the labors of Hercules, silver and bronze vessels, clay lamps, a cup of cast—rather than blown—glass (a remarkable advance for the first or second century A.D.), busts of Roman emperors and an ivory doll that came from the tomb of a little girl who was buried near the Roman Basilica of St. Sebastian.

These are among the smaller treasures of the Etruscan Museum. In the nearby Room

Column Crater decorated with episodes from the Trojan War, Corinthian, ca. 575 B.C. Astarita Collection.

ABOVE *Kylix with Oedipus and the Sphinx*, painted in the manner of Douris, ca. 480–470 B.C.
RIGHT *Votive Statuette of a Boy*, from Tarquinia, second century B.C., bronze.

of the Bronzes stands the half-life-sized centerpiece of the collection: the *Mars of Todi*, a bronze statue of the fifth century B.C. Found buried beneath four slabs of travertine in the Umbrian town of Todi in 1835, it was one of the *raisons d'être* for the museum that was inaugurated twenty months later. Roncalli terms it "one of the five or six most important bronzes preserved from pre-Roman Italy and one of the few large ones to survive." It represents a young warrior leaning on a lance with his left hand and offering a libation with a cup that should be in his right hand but is instead exhibited in a showcase to his right. The cup, found only recently by Roncalli in another showcase of the Etruscan Museum, was at first attached to the hand, but the statue is so inviting and appealing that visitors tended to touch the cup. The back of the warrior's head is missing, too, but that has to do with neither vandalism nor combat: the gold helmet he originally wore has been lost. The inscription on his armor, *"Ahal Trutitis dunum dede,"* is simply an acknowledgment—in early Umbrian (an Indo-European dialect of Italy), not Etruscan—of the man who commissioned the statue: "Ahal Trutitis gave this as a gift."

Near the *Mars of Todi* are two bronze statuettes of boys, both smiling and seated with their left legs curled beneath them. Although such *ex voto* offerings were not uncommon in Etruria in the first and second centuries B.C., most were made of terracotta and not expensive bronze. In the nearby Room of the Terra Cottas is a rare portrait bust of a woman. She is smiling, perhaps because women had equality in ancient Etruria or else because the Etruscans, like the Greeks, adhered to what art historians call the "archaic smile," which animates the face by upturning the corners of the lips.

Between the sixth and third centuries B.C.,

mirror-making was a major art of Etruscan handicraft, and many bronze mirrors brighten the showcases around the *Mars of Todi*. In particularly good condition is one from Vulci dating from around 470 B.C. with a relief showing the dawn goddess Eos (Aurora in Roman myth) abducting the handsome young hunter Cephalus from Mount Hymetus to Syria. The relief technique used here is rare; engraving was much more common. And the ivy branch around the rim of the mirror is inlaid with silver.

The Vatican Museums were among the first in the world to found their own scientific laboratories, back in 1923, for the preservation and restoration of works of art as well as for the detection of forgeries. (Only one fake has been unmasked in the many collections: a *Holy Family*, purportedly painted by Murillo and presented by a queen of Portugal to a pope during a royal visit to the Vatican a century ago.) Today, nobody in the Vatican works more closely with the labs than Etruscologist Roncalli. First and foremost is the chemotherapy that keeps bronzes, which are preserved when compressed within soil for centuries, from decomposing after exposure to air. Once a bronze is pronounced free of impurities, it is coated with *benzotriazolo*, which chief scientist Nazzareno Gabrielli says "does for the bronze what pincers do for a lobster: it keeps the bronze from accepting any new substance, but allows it to breathe."

Only then can the detective work that Gabrielli enjoys most begin. With bronzes found in Etruria, he can pinpoint the century and place of origin, sometimes even the actual workshop: "Bronze is made of copper and tin. The Etruscans used the copper by itself and then added tin to it. The Romans introduced lead. So, with chemical analysis, we can say this piece is surely from the Etruscan period while that one is Roman."

ABOVE *Funeral Carriage*, from the Regolini-Galassi Tomb, Cerveteri, second half of the seventh century B.C., bronze and wood.
BELOW The Room of the Biga takes its name from the Roman chariot, or biga, that is its centerpiece. Only the marble body of the chariot is ancient. The rest was restored in the late eighteenth century.

Pair of Armlets, from the Regolini-Galassi Tomb, Cerveteri, first half of the seventh century B.C., gold.

Sometimes archeologist Roncalli starts out with a scientific study and then uses it in his stylistic analysis. He recently presented Gabrielli with more than a hundred bronze mirrors for dating and tracing. Once Gabrielli had sorted them chronologically and geographically, Roncalli studied them stylistically to see what artistic links were suggested or documented by Gabrielli's analysis.

More often, the archeologist turns to Gabrielli to confirm his conclusion—as, for example, when Roncalli's stylistic eye matched up the vase and lid by Exekias in different parts of the Etruscan collection and Gabrielli's tests verified the linkage.

With the *Mars of Todi*, both methods were used: Roncalli's artistic research dated the statue to between 400 and 390 B.C. and Gabrielli's scientific analysis fixed it in the same period of purity in Etruscan art. Roncalli, however, was uncertain whether the existing statue had been made at one time from head to toe. Gabrielli's chemical anaylses found the statue so homogeneous in bronze components that it had to have come out of one workshop in a short span of time.

A room away from the *Mars of Todi* another reason for the founding of the Etruscan Museum in 1837: the contents of the Regolini-Galassi Tomb, unearthed in 1836 outside Rome just south of Cerveteri, where the emptied tomb can still be visited. (General Vincenzo Galassi directed the dig and Alessandro Regolini was the archpriest of the area.) One of the wonders of the Vatican, the Regolini-Galassi Tomb has the welcoming air of a living room, even though its furnishings are exhibited behind glass. It stands, says Roncalli, "as a kind of parenthesis within the museum: a tomb that existed practically untouched and was excavated quite correctly by even the most modern criteria. So here you have one of the world's most complete witnesses to the Etruscan culture of the seventh century before Christ."

The tomb had at least two occupants. One was a woman of noble birth whose bronze throne and jewelry—including a superb gold fibula (a forerunner of the safety pin) embossed with ducks and lions—one sees upon entering the room. The second was surely a man of equal rank whose war carriage is the tomb's centerpiece and whose funeral bed, at the far end, is a rare example in bronze of a type more commonly made in stone. But there is a slight possibility that a third person, who was cremated, was also buried in the tomb. Perhaps he was the trusted warrior of the nobleman who lay on the funeral bed.

Both the war carriage and funeral bed have wheels, but the rims of the war carriage wheels are smoothed from use, while those of the funeral bed are studded with iron to brake it into solemn slowness for its one trip to the grave. Amidst this treasure trove in which he loves to linger among fibulae and breastplates, parade shields and amphorae, Roncalli singles out one of the

RIGHT An ancient bronze pinecone gives the Court of the Pigna its name.

BELOW Scene from the base of the lost Column of Antoninus Pius, showing the *Apotheosis of Antoninus Pius and His Wife, Faustina*, Roman, late first century A.D., marble.

smallest but most important pieces in all of Etruscology: an ink pot made of *bucchero*, a local shiny black ceramic ware, inscribed with an alphabet that includes not just Etruscan characters but Greek and Phoenician letters, too. "There are also," Roncalli points out, "simple syllabifications of sounds like *ki-ko-ku*. It is a model learning alphabet, and its importance to Etruscology is that it is one of the earliest documentations of writing in Europe. There are very few documents dating back beyond the fifth century B.C." But the joy this ink pot gives Roncalli—who sees archeology in part as "contemporary history done by human beings"—comes from his awareness that the contents of an Etruscan tomb were always chosen by either the deceased (well in advance) or his survivors: "So I am sure that either the gentleman wanted to show he could write or else his family sent the alphabet after him. In either event, the ability to write was one of the gifts that he brought with him to the afterlife."

Leaving the Etruscan Museum by its main entrance, one comes next to the domed Room of the Biga, which takes its name from the two-horse chariot, or biga, that is its centerpiece. The carriage body, of ancient Grecian marble, once served as the papal throne in the Roman church of San Marco, but it was cleverly restored and embellished between 1786 and 1793 by the sculptor Franzoni (to whose flamboyant imagination we also owe the Pio-Clementine's Room of the Animals) with matching wheels, shaft and horses to take advantage of the throne's soaring, triumphal inspiration. Around it stand second- and third-century children's sarcophagi depicting cupids competing in cart races at the circus of life, a statue of Dionysos and several discus-throwers; one of them, a lesser copy of Myron's, comes from Hadrian's Villa. The other discus thrower, a

ABOVE *Ink Pot* inscribed with an alphabet that includes Etruscan characters as well as Greek and Phoenician letters, from the Regolini-Galassi Tomb, Cerveteri, second half of the seventh century B.C., *bucchero* ware.
OPPOSITE *Mirror* decorated with a winged and bearded diviner examining the liver of an animal, from Vulci, late fifth century B.C., bronze.

marble Roman copy from the first century A.D. of a bronze Greek original—probably by Naukydes—makes an interesting comparison with Myron's more famous version.

THE PINECONE AND THE BASE

Beyond the Room of the Biga, one can commit oneself to the long march to the Sistine Chapel via four major galleries and the Raphael Rooms or one can double back down the Simonetti Stairway and, from its foot, go left for a relaxing stroll through the Court of the Pigna, a former apple orchard. At one end, a temple facade actually belongs to the Braccio Nuovo (New Wing) of ancient statuary. At the opposite end, inside a three-story niche, stands the large bronze pinecone from which the courtyard takes its name. Made in Rome around the time of Christ, the cone once was a fountain in the cloister of the early Basilica of St. Peter, where Dante mentions seeing it in *The Divine Comedy*. In the early seventeenth century it was moved to this courtyard, which was restored and reopened to the public in 1981.

On the other hand, if we go right instead of left from the foot of the Simonetti Stairway, we will pass the sixty-four-ton marble base of a column erected in Rome's Piazza Montecitorio shortly after A.D. 161 by the Emperor Marcus Aurelius and his brother, Lucius Verus, to honor their adoptive father Antoninus Pius (86–161). Ornately carved with inscriptions and scenes glorifying Antoninus Pius and his wife, Faustina (104–141), the base survived a seventeenth-century Roman fire that destroyed its column, but it was badly damaged by the blaze as well as by centuries of neglect. Removed to the Vatican, it sat for many years in the Court of the Pigna until, in 1980, its transport to its present location proved a major feat of hydraulic lifting and engineering: two months in the planning, but just a weekend in the execution. And its subsequent rehabilitation by chief sculpture restorer Ulderico Grispigni was also a major feat of restoration along the lines developed in 1972 by Grispigni and his team to rescue Michelangelo's *Pietà*, an episode we will experience later in our odyssey.

THE GREGORIAN PROFANE MUSEUM AND THE PIO CHRISTIAN MUSEUM

IN 1963 POPE JOHN XXIII commissioned two new Vatican buildings to house three collections being moved from the Lateran Palace on the other side of Rome: one building for the Gregorian Profane and Pio Christian museums of antiquities; the other for a Missionary-Ethnological Museum founded relatively recently (1926). In 1965, however, Paul VI blocked construction of the second because too many buildings were sprouting in the Vatican Gardens. The Missionary-Ethnological Museum, therefore, was wedged into the same building as the other two Lateran transplants.

Externally, that building—begun by Vatican architects and completed by the brothers Fausto, Lucio and Vincenzo Passarelli, who won medals for the Italian Pavilion at Montreal's Expo '67—seems the wrong architecture in the wrong place. With its turrets slanted upward, only the sundial on its projecting cube keeps one from concluding that this is a mobile airport terminal poised for takeoff. Since the building works better inside than outside, a variation on an old Polish joke about Warsaw's Palace of Culture has been heard within the Vatican: "The best view of the Vatican Gardens is from the new museum building because from there you can't see the new museum building."

The Gregorian Profane Museum, which was opened to the public in 1970, takes its name from Pope Gregory XVI, who inaugurated it in the Lateran Palace in 1844. Its collection consists of sculpture from the Roman Imperial Age (first to third centuries A.D.), including Roman copies and versions of Greek originals from the classical age (fifth and fourth centuries B.C.). Most of the material comes from sites in the old Papal States.

The museum itself is actually one vast 4,800-square-yard room in which 621 works are grouped according to type, such as sarcophagi, urns, portraits and reliefs. The use of metal trellises for supporting walls and

OPPOSITE *Sophocles*, Roman copy of a Greek original of the fourth century B.C., marble.

LEFT *Head of Athena*, from the figure of the goddess shown below, known as the *Athena Lancellotti*.
BELOW A view of the Gregorian Profane Museum. The figures of *Athena* and *Marsyas* are Roman copies of Greek originals by Myron, fifth century B.C., marble.

iron pipes for pedestals provides a discreet background that gives full play to the marble sculpture.

Opposite the entrance are fragments of Roman marble copies of a famous bronze group, *Athena and Marsyas*, by the fourth-century B.C. sculptor Myron, creator of the *Discus Thrower*. An imperious gesture by the goddess Athena is preventing the nimble satyr Marsyas from snatching away her double flute. Some imagination must be brought to bear, as Marsyas is semi-emasculated and the double flute is missing.

One of the most impressive works here is the slightly larger-than-life statue of *Sophocles* (496–406 B.C.). Looming large and virtually intact amidst the maimed and mutilated muses and deities, the poet is presented in the prime of life, stone mantle draped about him as he gazes into the distance with an expression that is serene, contemplative, yet expansive, as if he were about to expound. At his right foot stands a basket of stone parchments, presumably his plays. This marble statue is probably a Roman copy of a lost Greek bronze original placed in the Theatre of Dionysos in Athens during the fourth century B.C. Found in 1839 at Terracina, it was presented to Gregory XVI by the Antonelli family.

Another highlight of the Gregorian Profane Museum is the *Chiaramonti Niobid*, a now-headless girl running, cloak flying in the wind, arms raised to ward off imminent disaster. She was one of the seven daughters of Niobe, who also bore seven sons and who, according to Homer in the *Iliad*, made the mistake of boasting about her fertility to the goddess Leto, who had only two children. But they were Apollo and Artemis, the "divine twins," who took the mortal Niobe's boast as an insult to their mother and slew all of Niobe's children with their arrows. This

Niobid takes her name from the Vatican's Chiaramonti Museum, her former home.

Nearer *Sophocles* than the *Chiaramonti Niobid* is the rim of a large floor mosaic reconstructed with fragments of another mosaic found in Rome in 1833 and dating back to the age of Hadrian (about A.D. 130). On one side are six theatrical masks and other stage props. On the other three sides are artistically scattered mosaic scraps left over from a banquet: chicken legs, fishbones, lobster claws, snail shells, husks, nutshells, fruit cores, leaves and other leavings. Each fragment casts its own mosaic shadow. And a mosaic mouse is gnawing a nut on the strip opposite the masks. This special type of still-life painted-pavement art is known by the Greek term *asaroton* or "unswept floor."

A detail of a historical relief shows a son welcoming his father to Rome in the year A.D. 70. In this historic homecoming, the father, hand raised in salute, is Vespasian, who had been proclaimed Roman emperor in Alexandria a year earlier, and the son is the despot Domitian, then the *urban praetor* (more commandant than magistrate) of Rome, who made the city ready for his father. This frieze was commissioned by Domitian, who later became emperor himself in A.D. 81 and whose reign of terror lasted fifteen years until his wife, Domitia, had him stabbed to death. In a second frieze portraying a departure of Domitian, his face has been replaced by that of his successor, Nerva, but the obliterated Domitian is still recognizable by his hairstyle. The arrival and departure friezes are known as the *Chancery Reliefs*, because they were unearthed between 1937 and 1939 beneath the Palace of the Apostolic Chancery in Rome's Campus Martius.

In a section of sarcophagi, we behold the fate that befell the fleeing *Chiaramonti*

Head of Marcus Aurelius, Roman, ca. A.D. 176, marble.

Niobid and her brothers and sisters. Amphon and Niobe watch with helpless horror as Apollo and Artemis, shooting from the lid of the coffin, slay the couple's children with arrows. Then, around the corner of the coffin, we glimpse the parents grieving at their children's tomb and are reminded of Hamlet's phrase, "Like Niobe, all tears." Nearby are two sarcophagi from the second and third centuries that are particularly well preserved, perhaps because their subject is *Bacchus*. Farther along is the front of a large sarcophagus showing philosophers and muses; the imposing, if noseless, central figure is thought to be the Neo-Platonist philosopher Plotinus, for the sarcophagus was carved shortly after his death in A.D. 270.

From the windows of the Gregorian Profane Museum we have been catching panoramic glimpses of modern Rome, including a luxury hotel and a less recent observatory. Now, at the circular west end of the building, we climb a staircase and, from the balcony, confront the Museums' most vivid view of the Vatican Gardens and the dome of St. Peter's. In two semicircular courtyards just below the balcony are third-century mosaic pavements from the Baths of Caracalla showing fierce athletes and rugged referees upon whom one would wisely fear to tread.

Good Shepherd, third or fourth century A.D., marble.

Chiaramonti Niobid, Roman, first century B.C., possibly copy of Greek original or the fourth century B.C., marble.

Omphale, ca. A.D. 200, marble.

Tomb Plaque of Severa, decorated with the *Adoration of the Magi*, from Rome, ca. A.D. 330, marble.

When you have crossed this balcony, you are in the Pio Christian Museum, founded by Pius IX in 1854, a couple of years after he created a Commission for Christian Archeology to supervise the excavation and maintenance of the Roman catacombs. Monuments of Early Christian art that couldn't be preserved *in situ* were transferred to the museum in the Lateran. Among the six hundred statues, mosaics, fragments and sarcophagi on display in this new setting is a particularly fine marble *Good Shepherd*, young and beardless with hair falling in long curls over his ears and a lamb borne on his shoulders. Dating back to the third or fourth century, it is one of the earliest representations of Christ extant— but as famous for its evocative force as for its historical value.

On the wall nearest the *Good Shepherd* are two fragments of the *Cippus of Albercius*, one of the most important Christian epigraphs in existence. Found in 1883 at Hieropolis in Phrygia (now part of Turkey), they were presented to Pope Leo XIII by the Sultan of Phrygia and the British archeologist who discovered them. The inscription was dictated by Bishop Albercius of Hieropolis during the reign of Marcus Aurelius (161–180), which crowns it as what historians call "the queen of Christian inscriptions": the most ancient work of its kind which can be dated to a reasonably specific time. "Faith led me everywhere," Albercius says in part, "and set before me to eat in every place fish from the spring, mighty and clean, which the spotless Virgin catches and gives us as food every day . . . and, together with it, a fine wine and, to mix with the wine, she offered us bread." This is the earliest datable documentation of the Eucharist, in which bread and wine are consecrated.

THE VATICAN LIBRARY AND THE HISTORICAL MUSEUM

THE VATICAN LIBRARY IS A separate organization within the Vatican, but it is a museum in itself and contains two museums of its own: the Sacred and the Profane. The Vatican Museums, in fact, were an offshoot of the Library and were at one time administered by the Library's prefect. While the Museums have had their own chief since the appointment of Antonio Canova as general inspector of fine arts by Pius VII in 1805, all art given to the Vatican still automatically goes first to the Library, which then offers its new acquisitions to the curators of the Museums. (Until World War II, the Library did not always deign to consult the Museums' curators; it simply gave or withheld at will.)

To a public bedazzled and fatigued by the Sistine Chapel, the Vatican Library often represents a fifth-of-a-mile-long exit corridor that must be traversed. This is a pity, for its many treasures are worth a morning of anybody's time—beginning, at the Sistine end, with another of the three chapels of St. Pius V. Built between 1566 and 1572, this one is lined with frescoes relating *Stories from the Life of St. Peter the Martyr*, painted by Jacopo Zucchi from designs by Vasari. In its showcases are objects from the treasury of the Sancta Sanctorum, which was transferred from the Lateran Palace to the Vatican in 1907. Priceless works in ivory, enamel and precious metals include a sixth-century ivory carved with the Healing of the Blind Man, once the lid of a case belonging to a physician, perhaps an oculist; the heads of Saints Peter and Paul from a seventh-century diptych; a complete ninth-century silver shrine, the crown jewel of which is the gold-leaf and enamel reliquary cross of Pope Paschal I, who reigned from 817 to 824; and an enameled eleventh-century Byzantine reliquary in which was later found the papal seal, also displayed, of the thirteenth-century Nicholas III.

Flanking this mid-level Chapel of St. Pius V are two Rooms of the Addresses, so named

OPPOSITE The Sistine Salon of the Vatican Library was built in the 1580s for Pope Sixtus V by the architect Domenico Fontana. According to tradition, a hundred painters worked on the elaborate decorations.

because the messages to and from the faithful of the world during the reigns of Popes Leo XII, Pius IX and Pius X used to be kept here. Today they house hundreds of church ornaments, vessels and vestments, including one of the world's finest collections of early textiles, some of them from the Sancta Sanctorum. A few of these woolen and linen tunics date back to the first three centuries after Christ, and several fragments of cloth still bear traces of the blood of Christian martyrs. One notable Sancta Sanctorum textile treasure is a thirteenth-century English cope, worn by a priest when celebrating Mass.

Off to the left of the second Room of the Addresses is a charming indoor oasis called the Room of the Aldobrandini Wedding because it houses a large first-century fresco of wedding preparations that once belonged to Cardinal Pietro Aldobrandini. Napoleon tried and failed to obtain this painting, but Pope Pius VII succeeded in 1818 and had it brought to this room built two centuries earlier. Its three ceiling frescoes of *Samson* are by Guido Reni (1575–1642), the Bolognese painter whose *Crucifixion of St. Peter* hangs next to Caravaggio's *Deposition* in the Pinacoteca.

The ancient, cracked fresco for which the Room of the Aldobrandini Wedding is named is an exquisite work showing Venus comforting a shrouded bride-to-be while others prepare a bath and perfumed oils for her. The rest of this wondrous room is adorned by mosaics found in Hadrian's Villa at Tivoli and on the Aventine Hill in Rome plus four fresco panels of the *Odyssey* from the first century B.C. taken, wall and all (rather than risk the transfer to canvas), from a home in Rome in 1833.

The Room of the Aldobrandini Wedding is a detour at the threshold of the Vatican Library's Christian Museum, here identified by its Italian name of Museo Sacro to avoid confusion with the Pio Christian Museum, already visited, The Library's Museo Sacro was created in 1756 by Benedict XIV "to increase the splendor of the City and bear witness to the truth of religion through sacred Christian monuments."

Its Room of the Papyri doesn't boast a single papyrus, for it no longer houses the Papyri of Ravenna (sixth to ninth century) for which Pius VI established it in the late eighteenth century. (These precious scrolls are displayed in modern showcases elsewhere in the Library.) What the room does offer are gilded glasses from the third to fifth centuries A.D. and even earlier fragments from the Roman catacombs. One of the early fourth-century glasses contains a full-length portrait of the mythical artisan Daedalus with six scenes of carpenters at work. Their saws and other tools have been executed to precise—and therefore historically valuable—detail. Just inside the next room is a showcase of medieval Byzantine icons, including a mosaic traveling icon from the twelfth or thirteenth century. Paying homage to St. Theodore, it is similar to those preserved in the monastaries of Mount Athos, the Vatican of Greece.

In the vast Gallery of Urban VIII, covered with cloths to protect them from light (nobody will tell you that the cloths can be lifted, but they can) are maps of the world going back to the twelfth century. Two copper maps of 1528 and 1529 show America as *Terra de Bacalaos* (Land of Codfish) on one and *Nova Gallia* (New Gaul) on the other.

In the second of the Sistine Rooms—a couple of chambers laid out by Sixtus V in the late sixteenth century to house papal archive documents and registers—stands a wooden device that resembles an instrument of torture wrought from a ship's wheel. It is

The Arrival of Odysseus in the Land of the Laestrygonians, from the fresco decoration of a Roman house of the first century A.D.

ABOVE *The Annunciation*, eighth century, silk.

OPPOSITE ABOVE Alessandro Algardi, *The Baptism of Christ*, terracotta model for a silver sculpture group for Pope Innocent X, ca. 1644.

OPPOSITE BELOW Gianlorenzo Bernini, terracotta models for sculpture groups: *Charity*, for the tomb of Pope Urban VIII, 1630; *Daniel in the Lion's Den* and *Habakkuk and the Angel*, for the Chigi Chapel, ca. 1655; *Charity*, for the tomb of Pope Urban VIII, 1630.

difficilia emergunt circa negocia
tionibus artis. Regimaus aucē đ
nisquicemp, nobikem bit cōsilī
ex sola suą nobilitate irra đe
detectorem q ad audioz fascim
prio ipin legi faciauct q pponi
mino baodcp ndulgtōrp nam
cum ars baur san nōīmbula p
pria qadmoītiq q tenere artuz
z nos non iachirembi in ceūna
itea Ltinoz uerba conentierai
onimbs q aūno iiā q mach
ndebanciem esse ppriet p quem
selleg posiit intento nřa Ei
bum deīnoru dania artę
itehmi us par
cum non
mp ueg the
one no pento
pnu precica mnenpat. Rinsus
hdam pars đ gēnerali cōscripū
ronet tam eōmz q spetant aq
expoīcam hm coz quē spetant
aq poīcerem oz nuqi uero đe
spoīalz consi deratōīse cozūde in
Intentio uero nra đ manifestan
in boc lizo đe uenatōē adūg
ea que sunt sicut sunt z ad ar
tis cerzsuidinem redigere quozū
nullo habuit sciam bacten⁹ neq
irem Modus agendi ē psai
cus proēmialis z execuūūer exe
cuūūos uero multipler partiū

none of these, but is rather a sixteenth-century embosser designed by Bramante for affixing the lead papal seal of authenticity to parchments issued by his office. After each pope's death, his seal was broken. Since this seal was called *bulla* in Latin or *bolla* in Italian, letters so sealed became known as papal bulls. Across the hall from Bramante's *bulla* stand an early twentieth-century version of the same device. Even heavier, it is shaped like scales of justice.

Here the gifts begin. Sprinkled among the exhibits of the Vatican Library's remaining rooms are presents to the popes over the past century or two: moon rocks from the astronauts; a silver and gold tabernacle from the Torino diocese; "mute swans of peace" in porcelain created by the Boehm Studio and presented to Paul VI by the Archdiocese of New York in the bicentennial year 1976; a green and gold cross from Russian royalty to Pius IX; a basin from the Duke of Northumberland; marble slabs given by the Austrian Republic to John XXIII and by Emperor Franz Joseph I to Leo XIII; and, most ironically, a candelabra used for the coronation of the Emperor Napoleon I that was given to Pius VII (Barnaba Chiaramonti), who spent much of his papacy (1800–23) retrieving the art treasures that Napoleon had taken off to Paris in 1797.

At the "tiniest prayer book," a sixteenth-century *Masses of Saints Francis and Anna*, perched atop the "largest prayer book," a thirteenth-century Hebrew Bible, turn right for the Sistine Salon, a long hall built by Domenico Fontana for Sixtus V from 1587 to 1589. Conceived as the Library's reading room, it has so much going on along its lush walls, pillars and ceilings that I defy anybody

OPPOSITE *Frederick II, Holy Roman Emperor*, from *De arte venandi cum avibus*, a treatise on falconry written by the emperor with supplements by his son Manfred, thirteenth century, parchment.

to read a book or even an illuminated manuscript in such surroundings: fresco after fresco created by a group of Mannerist painters led by Cesare Nebbia (1534–1614), who collaborated with Muziano on the Gallery of Maps ceiling. The Sistine Salon's lunettes are devoted to episodes from Sixtus V's papacy, one of intense building. The walls on one side depict libraries through the ages; on the other, ecumenical councils. The pillars honor the inventors of the alphabet, from Adam to Christ.

As if the Sistine Salon isn't a sight sure to boggle eyes already sore from the Sistine Chapel, its aisles are lined with more gifts and globes (additional ancient and medieval maps are displayed in an anteroom) and its showcases are filled with rotating exhibits from the Vatican's vast store of nearly 100,000 manuscripts and incunabula, which include an eighth-century Anglo-Saxon gospel; a fourteenth-century *Chronicle of Manasses* in Bulgarian; a thirteenth-century illustrated book of falconry by Frederick II, King of Germany, Sicily and Jerusalem; a tenth-century copy of the cookbook of Apicius, the first-century Roman gourmet who killed himself when he could no longer finance his feasts; letters, poems and drawings of Michelangelo; autograph poems of Petrarch; and letters of St. Thomas Aquinas, Raphael and, yes, Martin Luther. Recent exhibitions have featured Henry VIII's love letters to Anne Boleyn, signed "your loyal friend," and two manuscripts of Virgil's *Aeneid*, the *Vergilio Vaticano* and *Vergilio Romano*, from the fourth and fifth centuries A.D. These are the oldest known illustrated manuscripts of the Latin epic poem written shortly before the time of Christ.

Rejoining the marathon corridor at its halfway mark upon leaving the Sistine Salon, we pass more trophies in the Pauline Rooms

The Historical Museum, founded in 1973 by Pope Paul VI, houses papal vehicles. The most splendid, visible at right, is a grand berlin preceded by gilded angels bearing the papal insignia.

and then, in the Alexandrine Room, an eleventh-century linen altar cloth from the Sancta Sanctorum. The five-room Clementine Gallery features models and studies by Bernini, of whom, surprisingly, nothing else is on display within the Vatican Museums. The last two rooms of our trek through the Vatican Library comprise the Museo Profano, which Clement XIII founded in 1767 "to preserve the monuments of Roman antiquity." As with the Gregorian Profane Museum, which we have visited, "profane" means secular works of art: in this case, medals and coins as well as statues of secular beings and pagan deities. The Library's Museo Profano is, in fact, sometimes identified as the "Pagan Museum."

It is, however, not quite the "charming little Museo Profano" that Georgina Masson describes so enthusiastically in the 1974 edition of her definitive *Companion Guide to Rome*. To her, it "seems almost like the salon of a private house. Its great charm lies in the fact that its eighteenth century décor is complete, right down to the cases of rare

Brazilian wood designed by [Luigi] Valadier (1726–85), though it was only completed during the reign (1775–99) of Pius VI. The cases contain chiefly small Etruscan and Roman bronzes and Roman ivories. . . ."

To each his own, but to me the Museo Profano is a saddeningly looted and vandalized salon. Like the paintings and sculptures of the Pio-Clementine Museum, just a vestibule away, its rich collection was taken off to Paris in 1797, but hardly any of it was recovered. The Museo Profano's most precious coins and cameos had been cleverly concealed behind documents in ornamental cabinets, but even that didn't protect them. To make matters worse, what little is left is hard put to compete with a souvenir stand that has lately been added to the next-to-last room of the Vatican Library, effectively destroying any semblance of a salon.

Another view of papal history is offered by the Historical Museum, founded in 1973 by Pope Paul VI. Here, in a long subterranean coach house near the Square Garden, are kept the vehicles that the popes have used since the early nineteenth century.

The most splendid carriage here is the grand gala berlin (named after the German city where this kind of closed carriage was first made) built for Leo XII in the 1820s by the noted Roman coachmaker Gaetano Peroni and used by later popes for the next half-century. All red and gold, it is preceded by two child-sized golden angels bearing the papal crown and keys to the kingdom of heaven, in which are symbolized the pope's power as successor of St. Peter. The coachmen rode in back. One cannot imagine this lavish wagon being drawn by anything less than solid gold horses.

Behind the gala berlin (and dwarfed by it) are uniforms, flags and weapons of the papal armed forces (the last ceremonial vestige of which was disbanded in 1970 by Paul VI), the Knights of the Faith (disbanded with the advent of the Roman republic in 1798) and the Swiss Guards, who have been on the job as the pope's personal guardians ever since Julius II began recruiting them in 1505. Most notable in this collection is the gold-on-burnished-steel breastplate of Count Filippino Della Porta Rodiani, who served as "broken lance" (lanciaspezzata) to Pius VI toward the end of the eighteenth century. As a Knight of the Faith, a lanciaspezzata broke a ceremonial spear as his pledge to defend the pope to the death.

The parade of papal panoply ends with a reddish brown Citroën automobile used by Popes Pius XI and XII. The back seat is an ornate papal throne with red plush jump seats for His Holiness's entourage. The interior walls are inlaid with carved and painted saints and symbols. Exterior trappings include a blue sun visor, two spare tires mounted near the running boards and a pair of electric lanterns that look like little gas lamps.

THE MISSIONARY-ETHNOLOGICAL MUSEUM

"THERE ARE ONLY two other museums for the history of religion and they are both in the Soviet Union," says Father Jozef Penkowski, curator of the Vatican's Missionary-Ethnological Museum of religious artifacts. "One is in Leningrad and the other is in the old cathedral of Vilnius, Lithuania, where they have a miniature Court of Pope Pius IX from the nineteenth century. And I have heard that many of the visitors come not to learn about religion or affirm their atheism, but just to see what it is like in Rome."

The sardonic comment on Soviet travel restrictions typifies this Polish priest. A walk with him through forty centuries of religious objects and everyday artifacts is punctuated by eruptions of provocative prose and categorical observations.

"When I was called here to arrange this museum in 1967, I was told I should show off the biggest and the best from all over the world," Penkowski says. "But I answered: 'We are here in the Vatican, the capital of the Roman Catholic religion. Let's show at the Vatican the religious lives of other peoples who are looking for God—man in search of the divine!' That's why there is nothing of Europe in *this* museum."

The bulk of the museum's collection was acquired all at one time. For the 1925 Missionary Exposition in the Vatican, missionary congregations around the world lent their most treasured artifacts. When Pope Pius IX paid an official visit to the exposition, its organizer, Father Wilhelm Schmidt, a German priest who was the most famous ethnologist of the time and founder of the Institut Anthropos near Vienna, suggested that the temporary exhibition be converted into a permanent museum. The Holy Father accepted the idea and more than half of the congregations converted their loans into gifts. Much of the rest of the collection came from private donors. And there was considerable African and Asian art

OPPOSITE *Bust of a Creek Indian* is one of a collection of North American Indian portraits carved for the Vatican in the nineteenth century by Ferdinand Pettrich.

that the Vatican hadn't known what to do with after inheriting it from the defunct Borgia Museum in Velletri, near Rome, in the nineteenth century upon the death of the last Cardinal Borgia.

In 1926, a year after the Missionary Exposition ended, Pius XI and Father Schmidt founded the Missionary-Ethnological Museum in the Lateran Palace. There had been no problem finding Chinese and Hindu art; missionaries had long been buying and cherishing the former because it was exotic and the latter because it resembled Western art in its lifelike representations. But primitive African and Latin American art was another matter, for the artistic and anthropological value of implements and weapons had not been recognized by most missionaries. In shortest supply of all were religious cult objects. As Penkowski explains:

"Every so-called pagan who was converted to the Christian religion felt obliged to put away all of his old religious symbols, so he brought them to the missionary station. Some missionaries conserved them, but most were burned. I have the five oldest Colombian wooden sculptures in Europe: two masks, two supports and a statue. They were brought to Rome in 1692 by a priest just to prove that he had destroyed a pagan temple. Out of hundreds of objects, these five were all that were left.

"But I have a half-burned Zairian statue that was saved." Belgian missionaries, he says, were the first to recognize the esthetic merits of Congolese artifacts. What they didn't receive as gifts they often bought for packs of cigarettes or strings of beads. This is how the Museum of Central Africa in Tervuren, Belgium, was stocked, "though now Belgium is giving back a good fifty percent to the countries the missionaries took them from."

Padre Penkowski is a social anthropologist educated in Poland and Switzerland and trained in Tanzania. When he arrived in the Vatican, he accepted Pope Paul VI's decision to make his museum a joint tenant with the Gregorian Profane and Pio Christian museums as a blessing in disguise. The architects Passarelli presented Penkowski with only the outside walls and let him tell them how to fill in the inside: "The showcases were designed only after I decided what I wanted to exhibit. For the first time in Vatican history, content came first and the curator didn't have to fit what he had into a form that was designed centuries ago. There would be no long halls and a minimum of doors, just panels or twists-and-turns as you went from one culture to another —and yet it would all be one."

The museum is laid out on two levels. The main floor is for the general public, while objects of purely ethnographical significance are kept in an overhead maze of catwalks that are accessible to scholars. Both sections are divided into twenty-six geographical areas, either by country or by region.

The aim of the museum is definitely not to proselytize for the Vatican's faith—or, for that matter, any other. Proudly, Penkowski points out the two *Takuchai*—Chinese enamel guardian lions made in Peking in the nineteenth century—that flank the museum's subterranean entrance. The lion faces outward, while the lioness faces the interior. A number of Taoist visitors have objected that the lions are supposed to face in the same direction; if they don't, it's a bad omen. In fact, some Japanese and Chinese visitors have refused to enter the museum. But Penkowski insists, "I want to tell them this is a museum, not a temple. And it's better for the public to be able to see one lion from the front and the other from the back."

"In every area," says Penkowski, "I try to

ABOVE *Mask*, Karawari River, Papua, New Guinea, twentieth century, painted basketry.
OPPOSITE ABOVE *Figure of the God Rongo*, Gambier Islands, early nineteenth century, wood.
OPPOSITE BELOW *Figure of the God Tu*, Gambier Islands, early nineteenth century, wood.

show two things: first, the evolution of religious forms, from primitive to superior—in China, for example, from the cult of the dead and ancestor worship to Taoism and Confucianism. And second, the historical evolution or importing of other religions. Usually, in this sequence, Christianity comes last. For example, in China, Buddhism arrives around the beginning of the Christian era, then Islam in the eighth century, then Christianity later in the eighth century. The main exceptions are in North Africa, where Christianity precedes the Islamic religion, and the Near East, where Judaism and then Christianity precede the Muslim religion."

Penkowski is proud of the eccentricity of his Ethnological Museum. Pausing before a life-sized statue of a Chinese Madonna, he exclaims, as if meeting her for the first time: "I could never pray to this face! It looks like a geisha. She is Buddhist from the waist up, Christian from the waist down. And look at the peasanty European way she's cradling her child! Chinese women carry babies on their backs."

We are at a Christian altar adorned by a bronze statue of Father Marcellus Sterkendries, a missionary who saved the city of King Chow from extermination by the Mongols in 1911–12. To show their gratitude, the Christian converts of King Chow sacrificed their most valuable vases and had them melted down to make the statue. But Penkowski calls attention to the surrounding pillars. "Naked columns!" he says. "Chinese columns are always covered with dragons or flowers to keep the bad spirits away from the altar."

In Penkowski's China, there are tomb gifts dating back to the third century before Christ and a model of a pagoda from Fukien

enclosed in a circular niche almost like a phone booth in lower Manhattan's Chinatown. Perhaps most important of all is an exact reproduction of the altar of Confucius from his pagoda at Küfu, where he was born and buried. Confucius, smiling through two painted front teeth, is holding a tablet of honor that is the imperial scepter of dominion in the reign of thought. Over him is a gilt tablet inscribed: "Spiritual throne of Confucius, master of holy doctrines." This altar reproduction was made by Chinese artists in 1934–35 with permission from the philosopher's descendants.

Near a life-sized *Kwanyin*, a Buddhist fertility goddess from the Ming Dynasty (1368–1644) with a tiny Christlike child in the palm of her hand, Penkowski is inspired to take up a new theme that carries us from China all the way through the Third World: "God is not man or woman. God is spirit!"

He goes on to explain: "Our concept of God is Semitic. In the Old Testament, he is identified with a man. In Christianity, there is still God the Father. But, in the other religions, God often has elements of man and woman. Look at these ritual drums from Togo," Penkowski says. "Always in Africa, one drum is male and the other is female, even if both drummers are men. And wars are fought to possess these drums. When one tribe or village captures the other's drums and beats them loudly, the war is won and the fighting stops."

Before our two-hour walk around the world is over, we have looked at drums made of human skulls, flutes made of human bones, crucifixes from Melanesia and a painted wooden Madonna that is "the earliest Christian sculpture of the Solomon Islands: it dates back to right after the Second World War." From New Guinea there is a raised Hut of the Spirits for initiation rites and ancestor-worship. While telling me that all

OPPOSITE *Hut of the Spirits*, from New Guinea, was used for initiation rites and ancestor worship.

the relics adorning the hut (including five painted human skulls, torture instruments, plumed lances and sacrificial vessels) are authentic and only the thatched roof was made in Europe, Padre Penkowski falls to his hands and knees and, at a command from him, so do I. "Look!" he says. "This hut is for men only. The village women are forbidden to enter. But what is holding up the hut off the ground? One pillar—and it is carved as a statue of a woman. Talk about symbols!" He adds that two showcases of New Guinea sculptures represent the only religious art systematically and consciously collected for what became the Missionary-Ethnological Museum: "A German missionary named Father Kirschbaum, who was a collector, went out to New Guinea and gathered up a comprehensive set of

ancestors and spirits with the deliberate intention of presenting them to Pope Pius XI."

The New World welcomes us with a hut used for initiation rites in Tierra del Fuego and a model of Columbus's flagship, the *Santa Maria*. On the Mexican plateau, a small reddish stone statue of a feathered serpent is introduced by Penkowski as the god Quetzalcoatl: "For sacrifices to this god, the Aztecs would cut with a stone the breasts of young boys and girls and throw the beating hearts before this little statue. One of the reasons I think their civilization was destroyed so easily was that it was so much theocratic. It was governed by priests—no politicians, no economists—and so many people were destroyed early as sacrifices that the society had no resistance."

One of the oldest pieces of Americana is the shell-shaped wooden lectern, decorated with mother-of-pearl appliqués, that was used by Fra Bartolomeo de las Heras, chaplain of Columbus's voyages. Then, in the North American section, there is a familiar-looking statue of the death of Tecumseh. "This one is also in Washington," Penkowski says. "At the entrance to.the Smithsonian. Diplomatically, we say both are original. But, if you interrogate me, I must tell you ours is the older original."

Most of the busts in the United States section were sculpted by Ferdinand Pettrich (1798–1872), a German disciple of the Danish sculptor Albert Bertel Thorvaldsen (1770–1844), who settled in Rome in 1797. Thorvaldsen sent Pettrich across the Atlantic

in 1835 to bring back some new faces to the Vatican. Pettrich crossed the continent making sketches for these sculptures, which he subsequently executed in Brazil and then donated to Pius IX. "The Smithsonian has made a complete photographic and archivistic documentation of our Pettrichs," Penkowski says. One of the American Indian faces, though, doesn't look very Indian. In fact, his name was Rowly McIntosh and he was a Scotsman who became a chief of the Creek Indians.

Following yellow arrows through a labyrinth of time and places, we re-emerge in the Middle East of twenty centuries before Christ when we confront a clay tablet with cuneiform writing. Then we are in the Hebrew section that Father Penkowski created in 1971 after simply reminding his

OPPOSITE LEFT *Openwork Board*, Kamandimbit, Central Sepik River, New Guinea, twentieth century.
OPPOSITE RIGHT *Quetzalcoatl*, feathered serpent god of the Aztecs, Mexico, early sixteenth century, stone.
RIGHT *Auracos Figure*, Colombia, late seventeenth century, wood.

Painted wood *Madonna and Child*, made soon after the Second World War, is the earliest known Christian sculpture from the Solomon Islands.

superiors that Judaism, as the oldest existing Western religion and forerunner of Christianity, belonged in the museum just as the New Testament does not exclude the Old. When permission was granted, he bought five pieces in Jerusalem, including a fourteenth-century Torah scroll and seventeenth-century wooden case. A parchment *megillah* telling the story of Esther was purchased from Moshe Dayan; the soldier-statesman was also a passionate archeologist. The Hebrew collection's other *megillah*, a bridal gift in a silver case, "was the only object here that existed in the Lateran," Penkowski says, "but, after Pope Paul died, in making the usual inventory of the Papal Apartments, they discovered these two *menorahs* [candelabra] stored away and gave them to us." (Paul VI also left the Vatican Museums, as a private legacy, a group of thirty large statues dating back to the fourteenth century, that he apparently collected and bought from Roman antiquities dealers. All are being restored for a future exhibition.)

"How does the Torah fit into this museum's concept?" I ask.

"It is the first five books of the Bible," Penkowski replies, "and most important to all that follows. But I have to admit that the Near East section is the one that is discussed the most in the notes we find in the suggestion boxes, mostly from Americans. Your American Muslims [Penkowski guesses they are black] are complaining that the Torah is displayed and the Koran is not. Well, the Koran *is* displayed, but in the section of India [a nineteenth-century Koran from Agra, site of the Taj Mahal]. And my answer to all those who say the Koran should be displayed in the Near East section near the Torah is, 'Give me an old and worthwhile example of the Koran and I will display it.' "

The section on missionary synthesis, meaning Christian art from mission countries, includes a seventeenth-century Vietnamese version on canvas of the *Last Judgment*, a twentieth-century Vietnamese tabernacle in lacquered and gilded wood and a *Last Supper* in Chinese ink on white silk, painted by Wang-Su-Ta for the 1925 Missionary Exposition. This section is heralded, a little confusingly, by a lovely, richly gilded, pagodalike Christian altar, carved in Japan in the 1930s, which is placed opposite the Hebrew section. Only a small reflecting pool punctuates this sudden switch from Middle to Far East.

Back in his office, Penkowski shows me a long, slender wooden cross bearing a bronze black Christ. Pope John Paul II brought it back from Upper Volta. And Penkowski rejoices that Paul VI and John Paul II were the first popes to travel outside Italy since 1812, "for, upon their return, my office fills up like a Christmas tree with the relics they bring back from Brazil or Africa or North America. And, even when the pope stays here, I can take my pick of the gifts the visiting bishops and heads of state bring him. Look at this feather bonnet! He got it from your Canadian Iroquois Indians—and he wore it, too!"

The Missionary-Ethnological Museum takes tourists by surprise and then delight. But there is one public Penkowski says it hasn't reached "and that is the Italians. Oh, the northern Italians are rather cosmopolitan and they're all right about it, but the ones from Florence on down are too ethnocentric to deserve an ethnological museum. They have the mentality that what is not Italian or Mediterranean is barbarian. There was one old lady just the other day who came over to me without knowing I worked here and said: 'Father, would you believe that they have such heathen objects right here in the Vatican?' "

COLLECTION OF MODERN RELIGIOUS ART

AFTER NAPOLEON AND later Garibaldi reduced the Vatican State to an enclave of Rome, the Church—still rich in treasure but reluctant to reach out as it once had to embrace the great painters and sculptors of the time—loosened its link with living art for nearly a century. But soon after Cardinal Giovanni Battista Montini became Pope Paul VI in 1963, he gave a Mass for an assemblage of artists in the Sistine Chapel, where he told them bluntly: "We need you. Your art is precisely that of snatching its treasures from the heaven of the spirit and clothing them anew with words, color, with form, with accessibility. The friendship between Church and artist must be re-established."

Candidly, he confessed: "We bear a wound in the heart when we see you intent on certain artistic expressions which offend us, particularly when you separate art from life." But he went on to add: "We recognize that we, too, have caused you to suffer somewhat. You have been told that we have a certain style to which you must adapt yourselves; that we have this tradition to which you must be faithful; that we have these masters whom you must follow; that we have these canons from which there is no escape. We ask your pardon!" And then he asked, "Will the pope again become the artist's friend?"

That there was nothing rhetorical about this remarkable statement became apparent during the next decade, when papal envoys quietly approached galleries, connoisseurs and artists around the globe for donations of works to the Vatican Museums. In the United States, the tax-exempt Committee of Religion and Art of America (which later became the Friends of American Art in Religion, Inc.), headed by Terence Cardinal Cooke of New York, was founded in 1971 and spent more than half a million dollars acquiring some thirty American paintings and sculptures. Nowhere in the world, however, were any church funds used for the acquisitions, which included ten paintings, fifty-three etchings and a stained-glass window by Georges Rouault and another by

OPPOSITE Henri Matisse, *Tree of Life*, maquette for stained glass window for the Chapel of the Rosary of the Dominican Sisters at Vence, 1949, cut and painted paper on cardboard.

Fernand Léger. As the gifts of art flowed in, Pope Paul had some of them sent up from the storerooms to his private apartments to contemplate while dining. The Holy Father's hobby, *Newsweek* revealed, was modern art.

But the boldest move came in housing the new Collection of Modern Religious Art. The pope allocated fifty-six rooms that form a crown around the Sistine Chapel in the oldest parts of the Apostolic Palace. They include the Tower of Innocent III, whose reign began in the twelfth century, and the Borgia Apartment of Alexander VI (the Spaniard Rodrigo de Borja y Doms, father of Cesare and Lucrezia Borgia). Although the apartment had been left vacant for many years and had later been used for showing minor nineteenth-century objects, the idea of displaying Matisse, Manzù and Marino Marini beneath Pinturicchio ceiling frescoes shocked even many modern sensibilities.

Amazingly, the combination worked. There is little culture shock when you step from the Raphael Rooms into the Room of the Sibyls, where Cesare Borgia is said to have had his brother-in-law murdered. For there in the entranceway are Rodin's *The Thinker*, a Lello Scorzelli bronze statue of Pope Paul VI and a stunning 1943 oil, *Man Crucified*, by Ottone Rosai. To see this poor, ugly man in a cheap suit on a cross with factory smokestacks and a burning city in the background is to instantly identify the suffering of Christ with the suffering of modern man.

How was this miracle of accommodation wrought? Partly, curator Mario Ferrazza confides, it was done by putting bronze and marble busts as well as church-door panels (from competitions to decorate St. Peter's and Milan's Duomo), rather than paintings, into the gaudier Pinturicchio rooms—thereby minimizing color clashes. Besides, frescoes and modern art blend far better than do frescoes and ancient statuary in some other halls of the Vatican. Even critics who complained about the collection when it opened in 1973 were virtually unanimous in agreeing that modern art looked splendid in the Borgia Apartment. Critic Emily Genauer, for example, wrote that the Borgia Apartment was "very nice indeed" with "rooms of soaring ceilings, great sculptured mantels, frescoes by the fifteenth-century Pinturicchio [that] co-exist most attractively with the new twentieth-century tenants, perhaps even better than some of the twentieth-century works co-exist with each other." Still, she had to admit that "nothing quite prepares you" for it because, while "your admiration for Henry Moore, Jacques Lipchitz, Paul Klee, Ben Shahn, Jack Levine, Vasily Kandinsky, Abraham Rattner, Max Weber, Rufino Tamayo, John Sloan, Francis Bacon may be boundless . . . it's still a shock to find them displayed a wall away from Michelangelo."

Moore is represented by a 1954 watercolor sketch for a Crucifixion sculpture; Lipchitz by an undated bronze *Mother of Sorrows*; Klee by a linear 1925 watercolor, *City with Gothic Cathedral*; Shahn by nine paintings and a drawing as well as a tapestry, *Bring Back My Sons and Daughters*; Levine by a sepia-toned *Cain and Abel*; Kandinsky by a woodcut procession called *Sunday*; Rattner by three oils: *Pietà* (1958), *Crucifixion* (1964) and *Temptations of St. Anthony* (1945); Weber by a prayerful 1919 oil, *Invocation*; Tamayo by a pair of 1959 lithographs depicting *Riders of the Apocalypse*; Sloan by a 1922 oil, *Indian Religious Dance*; and Bacon by a large 1961 oil, *Study for Velazquez Pope*.

Ferrazza doesn't like to have to define "religious art." He says simply, "Our art doesn't limit itself to liturgical concepts of a religious idea. Certainly, Catholicism isn't

LEFT Giacomo Manzù, *Adolescence (Portrait of Francesca Blanc)*, 1940–41, bronze.
ABOVE Carlo Carrà, *The Daughters of Lot*, 1940, oil on canvas.

138

OPPOSITE Georges Rouault, *Holy Face of Christ*, 1946, oil on paper.
LEFT Graham Sutherland, *Study for the Crucifixion*, 1947, oil on hardboard.
BELOW Francis Bacon, *Study for Velazquez Pope*, 1961, oil on canvas.

inferred, as Jack Levine's and Ben Shahn's works bear witness. No, the core is that some religious spiritual philosophy motivated these artists. Sometimes, if we have religious work by an artist, we'll accept a donation that isn't religious because it is part of the total context of his work. On the other hand, there are Crucifixions, for example, that we decline because, while mechanically religious, they have no real spiritual content."

Since its inauguration, the collection has doubled to nearly 1,500 works, including graphics. Newer donations include a Jacob Epstein lead *Madonna and Child*; a bronze head by Giacometti; a twisting, soaring Lipchitz bronze, *Between Heaven and Earth*; designs created by Matisse for his Ste Marie du Rosaire chapel in Vence, near Nice, to join those already in the collection; three handsome Mirko bronzes and a mosaic; a 1907 Mondrian oil-on-cardboard landscape; a Reuven Rubin oil, *The Miraculous Fish*; a Rufino Tamayo oil, *Man and the Cross*; and an Utrillo oil-on-canvas Montmartre scene to join his four paintings of churches already in the collection. Recent Polish history, in which the Vatican emerged as a factor, is reflected by the donation of a snowy Jerzy Wolff oil, *Three Magi*, given by the late Stefan Cardinal Wyszynski, and a symbolic wood sculpture by Antoni Rzasa (1919–80) of a pilloried man donated by Edward Gierek before he was disposed as Communist Party leader in 1980.

Ferrazza begins a private tour of his collection in an anteroom off the Borgia Apartment's Room of the Sibyls—with Matisse chasubles and designs for his chapel in Vence, in the south of France. The vestments are under glass, but this is not enough to preserve them properly, for light is most destructive to textiles. Ferrazza explains: "There is a very fine invisible protective film painted on the glass to prevent any loss of color. As an extra precaution, there is a curtain on the window and the room's lighting can be adjusted to the intensity of the sunlight coming in." Sharing that Matisse anteroom are two small Rodin bronzes and a small Goya watercolor *Apostle* which, Ferrazza says, is also susceptible to light. One of the bronzes is a bust of *Pope Benedict XV*; the other, of a man and a woman intertwined upon a hand, is called *The Hand of God*, a theme that Rodin explored repeatedly.

The Room of the Creed's stately, solemn ceiling of prophets, apostles and scrolls is enlivened from below by an animated alabaster 1961 *Pietà* of Romano Rui; two joyous 1973 bronze centerpieces by Egidio Giaroli, *Noah's Ark* and *Tower of Babel*; a vivid 1970 oil, *Singing Roosters*, by Bruno Cassinari; and a 1926 marble bust of *Pope Pius XI* by Adolfo Wildt.

The Room of the Liberal Arts (with Astronomy, Grammar, Dialectic, Rhetoric, Geography, Arithmetic and Music enthroned as female figures in the lunettes overhead) lives in harmony with modern sculptures by Luciano Minguzzi and a *Crucifixion* surrounding a bronze pillar by the sculptor Giuseppe Pirrone honoring the Old and New Testaments.

The Room of the Saints, with the hand of Pinturicchio most in evidence (some frescoes in other rooms are products of his workshop), matches up brilliantly with twenty bold and golden bronze sculptures by Francesco Messina. Pinturicchio's frescoed saints include *Sebastian*, *Catherine*, *Paul the Hermit*, *Anthony Abbot*, *Juliana* and *Barbara*, as well as the biblical episode of *Susannah and the Elders*. Lucrezia Borgia was reputed by many (but refuted by Ferrazza) to have been Pinturicchio's model for *St. Catherine of Alexandria*, patron saint of the University of Paris and protector of

Mario Ferrazza, curator of the Collection of Modern Religious Art.

students and philosophers. Messina's bronzes of *Magdalen, Lazarus* and various saints and Old Testament figures are sinewy, dynamic works from the second half of the twentieth century, closely tied to the classical tradition in technique and subject matter.

In the Room of the Mysteries, below portraits of the Borgias and busts of the prophets, the bronzes of Lucio Fontana (1899–1968) penetrate the vast vaulted space with their own violent force.

In the Room of the Pontiffs, conceived for official papal ceremonies and boasting a ceiling stuccoed with grotesques by Perin del Vaga and Giovanni da Udine, an Aligi Sassu 1943 oil, *Descent from the Cross*, reminded Ferrazza of a wartime scandal in Italy's flirtation with modern art, when the Bergamo Prize competition refused to consider a Crucifixion by the Sicilian artist Renato Guttuso because it included a naked woman despairing beneath the cross. As a protest,

Sassu tried to withdraw his fully clothed *Desposition* out of sympathy with his fellow artist—and it is this one which wound up in the Borgia Apartment. Guttuso's partly nude Crucifixion never made it to the Vatican, though two other Guttusos are in Ferrazza's collection: a 1965 *Hand of Christ Crucified* and a 1973 view of the *Colosseum*.

"It's very clear that in the 1940s neither Italy nor the Vatican was ready for such art as Guttuso's Crucifixion to be put on display," Ferrazza said. But policy in the Vatican changed sometime after 1957, when Bruno Saetti did his tempera-and-charcoal *Nativity*, featuring a nude Madonna, that now hangs one Borgia Apartment room away from Sassu.

The six private audience rooms of Alexander VI are closed to the public when Pope John Paul II uses them for ceremonies, conclaves and small audiences (with royalty, prelates and diplomats) or while donning vestments for special services in the Sistine Chapel. There had just been one such Mass and the six rooms were still closed to the public, though not to Ferrazza. A portal by Bernini led us into a room with a wardrobe closet by Bernini, known as the Second of the Vestments. "The Holy Father has held several small audiences here in the last few days," Ferrazza remarked, adding that the room was also serving as a temporary resting place for two large new acquisitions that he hadn't yet been able to fit into permanent niches: larger-than-life wood sculptures by Marino Marini and Floriano Bodini.

The Marini was a *Cavalier*, an early (1936–37) example of a virile horse and nude rider. The Bodini, by one of the younger artists (born 1933) in the collection, was a 1968 sculpture of Paul VI liberating a dove from beneath his robes. Epic, almost

ABOVE Ben Shahn, *The Burial Society*, 1944, tempera on paper.
RIGHT Ottone Rosai, *Man Crucified*, 1943, oil on canvas.

unflatteringly monumental and beaky, like the prow of a ship, this portrait has been exhibited all over Europe.

I was remarking that the hands, with their elongated fingers, were absolutely hypnotic —when Ferrazza suddenly leaned and then lunged closer. Down by the pedestal, he had found a sliver, not much larger than a splinter, of wood and he traced it upward to the pope's right index finger.

"How lucky the rooms were closed," he said, "and I found it before somebody kicked it away. But how strange it should break off like that!" Ferrazza peered closer, touched the damaged finger, and it came off in his cupped hand. It took him a while to recover from the shock, but then he said, "Fortunately, the artist is living in Milan. I'll give it to the restorer and we'll invite the artist down to work with us. So it is not irreparable."

He tucked both pieces of finger into the breast pocket of his jacket. The big piece stuck up like a cigar. Ferrazza tried to go on with the tour, but when he turned the finger of Pope Paul over to a guard, everything stopped—or, rather, started. Because it happened on his beat, the guard registered even more distress than Ferrazza. He radioed for his captain, who made a report and took the two pieces of evidence.

By mid-afternoon, the scientific labs and the security forces had established that there were no fingerprints except Ferrazza's. X-rays of the evidence indicated that the broken sliver of finger had "impacted" from a heavy jolt that must also have weakened the hold of the glue joining finger to hand. "So we suspect," said security chief Vittorio Rossetti, "that someone who was helping the Holy Father dress knocked into it. Now we're compiling a list of everybody who was in that room and we'll be asking friendly questions in the interest of documenting the art

object's history. Surely it was done innocently, so nobody is going to get in any trouble for it, but we like to find out as much as we can. Best of all, none of the wood is missing. It was a clean break that can be fixed easily."

Which it was—by Vatican Museums technicians after the artist elected to leave the job to them. Today, Bodini's *Paul VI* stands in a place of honor in the Borgia Apartment's Room of the Pontiffs. The Marino Marini, however, went in the opposite direction, to the ground floor of the collection, where, ironically, the *Cavalier*'s left foot, which had disappeared before its donation to the collection, was still awaiting restoration at last viewing.

Beyond the Borgia apartment's thirteen rooms begin the *Salette Borgia*, fifteen more rooms on two floors. On the upper story is the Manzù *Chapel of Peace*, a light and airy, reverent yet exuberant room that many visitors consider the high point of the Vatican Museums Collection of Modern Religious Art.

Designed by the sculptor Giacomo Manzù down to the last gilded railing, prayer stool and knee-rest, the Chapel of Peace is considered his monument to Pope John XXIII, whose bust stands in the entranceway. Actually, the chapel honors an enlightened monsignor, Giuseppe de Luca, who brought sculptor and pope together in 1960 and died in 1962 of stomach cancer, the same disease that would attack Pope John a year later.

Built into de Luca's home in Rome in 1961, the chapel caught fire from an electrical mishap and was slightly damaged. Manzù took all the fixtures back to his workshop and had nearly finished restoring them when de Luca died. A little later, when the repair job was done, the monsignor's sister asked Manzù to install it in her home.

Giacomo Manzù's 1961 *Chapel of Peace* became a monument to Pope John XXIII.

The sculptor was reluctant, so at one of his portrait sittings with the pope, he consulted his friend. Addressing Manzù in the Bergamese dialect they shared, Pope John advised: "Don't give it to the family, because there's no priest in that house any longer. So sooner or later they'll be selling off his candlesticks, his crosses, his chalices and everything you've done—for there are many, many relatives to feed. Speak to my secretary about it."

Monsignor Loris Capovilla advised Manzù to donate the chapel to the Sisters of the Poor in Bergamo, and there it was installed in the room where the pope was born. But, a few years after Pope John's death, Monsignor Pasquale Macchi, private secretary to Pope Paul VI, phoned Manzù and said: "We have seen the chapel and would like to put it into the Vatican Museums."

Manzù replied: "It's not mine any more. You can do whatever you want with it." Though there were objections in Bergamo, just as there had been earlier in Rome when Manzù gave it to the Sisters of the Poor, the Chapel of Peace did indeed move to the Vatican in time for the inauguration of the Collection of Modern Religious Art in 1973. For its Vatican relocation, it required additional windows. When the Church offered to pay Manzù for the extra work he did, he declined the fee "because I don't want to mortgage the future of my soul." Still, the one time they met, Paul VI told Manzù: "You are the only artist today who could create a chapel."

Nowadays Manzù speaks of Paul VI fondly, but remembers his predecessor with love. The deep friendship between two strong personalities, both from Bergamo— the peasant Angelo Giuseppe Roncalli who became Pope John XXIII, and the shoemaker's son, Manzù, an atheist and communist who considers himself an artisan, not an artist—has been chronicled by Curtis Bill Pepper in his 1968 book, *The Artist and the Pope*. But even the opinionated Manzù didn't have an answer to a question that the pope posed the first time they met in the Papal Apartments, "Whatever happened between popes and artists? Why did the collaboration cease?" Later, in discussing religious themes for the bronze Doors of Death which Manzù designed for St. Peter's (the first new doors in the basilica for several hundred years), Pope John asked him: "Why don't artists today feel these things? Why is there this wall between us? Once there was a great river of religious art flowing through the Church."

John XXIII had a short-lived papacy (1958–63). Though his accomplishments were many, on this question at least there wasn't time to find an answer. To turn the tide, it took his successor, Paul VI, a conservator and consolidator, to create and crusade for art with the courage of his convictions and the passions of a connoisseur.

After the Manzù Chapel comes the Rouault Room, with his 1939 stained-glass *Crucifixion* plus half a dozen other works, of which the three oils—*Ecce Homo*, *Nazareth* and the *Sacred Heart*—possess much the same stained-glass glow. The next seven rooms offer an assortment of older modern artists (most born in the nineteenth century). One of the youngest is Salvador Dali (born 1904), who is represented by a 1960 oil, *Annunciation*, and an undated watercolor, *Sketch for an Altarpiece*, as well as the newly acquired 1977 *Enigma*. A fascinating colorist named Corrado Cagli (1910–76) catches the eye with three works in the Hall of the Pontiffs: a blue and gold mosaiclike tapestry of *St. George* standing triumphant over the dragon; a tapestrylike mosaic of *Christ and the Apostles*; and an encaustic (burnt-in with hot irons) tempera-on-wood painting of *Saints and Poets*. There is a room with six Chagalls, including a 1956 *Red Pietà* gouache, and a golden brown Gauguin *Religious Panel*, with a delicately primitive Crucifixion, on carved polychrome wood from the painter's first Tahitian odyssey (1891–93). Another room mixes half a dozen Utrillos with an Ossip Zadkine bronze, *Man with Guitar*, a 1916 Modigliani *Drawing of a Novice* and an uncharacteristic 1950 Vlaminck etching of a provincial church. Then come six rooms of Italian artists, including De Chirico and a *Madonna and Child* painted in 1962 by Carlo Levi, author of *Christ Stopped at Eboli*.

Four rooms with larger works follow, of which the most breathtaking room is the one with Léger's 1951 stained-glass window of the *Holy Tunic* flanked by four bronze evangelists. On the opposite wall is a golden bronze sunburst, *Pentecost*. The bronzes are all by the Neapolitan Lello Scorzelli, who lined both long side walls with huge, intricately detailed gilded-bronze processions representing the ecumenical councils Vatican I and II. They are led by Popes John XXIII and Paul VI, both kneeling in prayer. It is a room to remember.

The last of the four oversized rooms now houses Marini's *Cavalier*, seemingly charging at the same artist's soaring 1971 stone *Miracle*; Leonard Baskin's tender 1973 bronze *Isaac*; an eleven-and-a-half-foot-high Lucio Fontana stone *Madonna*; an eight-foot-high 1946 bronze Ivan Mestrovic *Pietà*; and a sixteen-and-a-half-foot-high 1962 tapestry of *Bethlehem* by Jean Lurcat (1892–1966). But all these giants are dwarfed by the sheer volume of eight large 1960–61 oil-on-canvas Bernard Buffets depicting *The Passion of Christ*.

The final twenty-three rooms are arranged primarily by nationality and begin with the U.S. donation of a room of Ben Shahns and continue through Europe with Oskar Kokoschka's nobly ironic postwar poster showing Christ reaching out to suffering children from a cross on which is written: "IN MEMORY of the CHILDREN of VIENNA WHO HAVE TO DIE of COLD and HUNGER this *Xmas*." Kokoschka (1886–1980) had this poster lithographed by the hundreds at his own expense, altering the language and location to fit each particular tragedy, which he raised funds to fight by selling the poster. This print was inscribed by the artist to Paul VI in 1969. Kokoschka is also represented by a 1972 watercolor still life of *Flowers*. Picasso's fish plates go almost unnoticed opposite a far more impressive 1971 John Piper oil-on-canvas night portrait of *San Moisé Parish Church*, *Venice*, dark green yet gleaming and so luminously mossy that you have to resist reaching out to touch.

Francis Bacon's *Study for Velaquez Pope* holds its own in a mostly Mexican room that features Orozco's 1944 *Martrydom of St. Stephen*; Tamayo's 1959 *Riders of the Apocalypse* lithographs; and two gaudy works by Siqueiros, a gutsy *Christ* (1970) and a gutted *Christ Mutilated* (1963), that almost, but not quite, overshadow a quiet Diego Rivera 1925 drawing of a *Church*. In an even lovelier intercontinental juxtaposition, the Argentine Raul Soldi's *The Virgin and Santa Ana* and the Japanese Inshò Domoto's 1974 *Madonna with Child* sit side by side, shedding new light and an old-fashioned tenderness seldom seen nowadays on time-honored themes. And they lead quite nicely into a section of Yugoslav naive paintings and a semiconcluding collage of fabrics that create an impressive *Church Interior*, the work of the Norwegian Jan Stangebye.

THE SISTINE CHAPEL

W HEN THE SISTINE Chapel was built and decorated five centuries ago, the schism between art and religion had not yet occurred and the papacy was a strong political power. All these elements are recorded in the Sistine Chapel, which takes its name from Pope Sixtus IV, who built it between 1475 and 1480. An early example of a multiuse structure, it was designed and built as both a chapel and a fortress to defend the Apostolic Palace from attack, a function seen in the battlements on the roof.

These political and religious purposes were expressed in the original frescoes painted on the walls, scenes from the lives of Christ and Moses. The events portrayed had the aim of stressing the role of Christ and his "precursor," Moses, as leaders of the people, legislators and priests. In Perugino's fresco of the *Handing Over of the Keys*, Christ symbolically transmits these roles to Peter, founder of the papacy, and to his successors. These frescoes of the lives of Christ and Moses were painted by some of the greatest artists of the time—Botticelli, Ghirlandaio, Pinturicchio and Piero di Cosimo as well as Perugino—and by themselves would have made the Sistine Chapel a magnet for art lovers. But twenty-five years after it was dedicated in 1483, Pope Julius II put Michelangelo to work painting the ceiling; and in 1536 Michelangelo returned to paint *The Last Judgment* on the wall behind the altar. For almost 450 years pilgrims have come, and they continue to come at the rate of a million and a half a year, to see the room which contains the greatest concentration of art in the world and in which the College of Cardinals elects new popes.

Inevitably the dust of centuries has mingled with the dust of pilgrims' shoes to dim the colors and details of Michelangelo and the other painters of the Renaissance. Periodic efforts at cleaning these frescoes in

OPPOSITE Michelangelo, *The Last Judgment*, 1536–41, on the altar wall of the Sistine Chapel. Restoration of *The Last Judgment* will not begin until the ceiling has been completed.

the past have usually darkened them at best and endangered them at worst. But the increasing pollution of Rome's air and the increasing number of visitors have accelerated the overlay of grime, and after evaluating the risks, the Vatican has undertaken the task of restoring these frescoes whose loss would rank with the destruction of Shakespeare's plays.

The restoration began in 1966 and is expected to take at least another dozen years. Only in 1980, however, had a restorer's skills been applied to the work of Michelangelo, and on February 10, 1981, the Vatican unveiled this crucial phase of its monumental conservation project.

It was a revelation to see the Sistine Chapel without scaffolding, and the east wall radiated a splendor that had been obscured for almost three centuries. Newly restored were portraits of five early popes, painted by Cosimo Rosselli, Domenico Ghirlandaio and others; two large frescoes, *The Resurrection of Christ* by Hendrick van den Broeck (also known as Arrigo Paludano) and *The Fight Over the Body of Moses* by Matteo da Lecce, both painted in 1571–72, almost a century later than the other twelve scenes from the lives of Moses and Christ that decorate the side walls of the chapel; and the *trompe l'oeil* "leather" curtain on the wall below them. But what everybody had come to see was Michelangelo's lunette depicting two of Christ's ancestors, *Eleazar and Mathan*, just below the ceiling. It was here that the restoration of Michelangelo's contribution to the chapel began.

Carlo Pietrangeli, director-general of the Vatican Museums, reinforced one's sense of the importance of the occasion when he welcomed the gathering. "In this holy place," he said, "in this unique and unrepeatable setting, authorities, scholars and the press have gathered here to see the results of the recent work of the Vatican Museums laboratory: the nearly completed restoration of an entire wall of the Sistine Chapel." The ceremonies also included a talk by Gianluigi Colalucci, who is solely responsible for those parts of the chapel painted by Michelangelo.

Because Michelangelo worked almost alone on the Sistine ceiling and the great *Last Judgment* on the altar wall, the Vatican hierarchy decided in 1978 that his work ought to be restored by one man rather than a committee. Their choice for the job was Colalucci, who at forty-eight had just become the Vatican Museums' chief painting restorer.

A good restorer doesn't paint, doesn't create, doesn't change a work of art, yet he does a little of all three. More than any other modern man, Colalucci is the first to see, to read, to penetrate the workings of Michelangelo's mind. But he would be the last to profess kinship with Michelangelo. He prefers to be regarded as a technician just doing a job and expecting to be neither applauded nor remembered for merely knowing his business. To be sentimental about his work could topple him from his lofty scaffold into the abyss of false perspective—a pitfall he avoided when I went up with him to look at his work in progress four and a half months before the unveiling of the east wall.

On a busy weekday in September 1980, Colalucci and I entered the Sistine, as everybody else does, through a door in the west wall, beneath *The Last Judgment*'s doomed souls—in fact, directly beneath the figure of Minos, the judge in Hades to whom Michelangelo assigned the features of Biagio da Cesena, Pope Paul III's master of ceremonies who had objected to the artist's painting naked saints in the Sistine Chapel. But we crossed over to the other side of the

RIGHT Exterior view of the Sistine Chapel, built for Pope Sixtus IV, 1475–81.

BELOW Gianluigi Colalucci, the Vatican Museums' chief painting restorer, working on the lunette of *Eleazar and Mathan*, Michelangelo's fresco.

ABOVE The newly cleaned lunette of *Eleazar and Mathan* blazes with color compared to the still dirty painting in the ceiling spandrel, *Judith Covering the Head of Holofernes*. Visible at bottom right is *Pope Marcellinus*, painted by Ghirlandaio.

OPPOSITE ABOVE Michelangelo, *The Fall of Man and Expulsion from Paradise*, from the ceiling of the Sistine Chapel, 1508–11.

OPPOSITE BELOW Also from the ceiling, *The Creation of Adam*.

west wall and stood beneath the scene of the dead being awakened for the Day of Judgment. On this side, the door below the fresco houses security equipment, including an electronic noise monitor and the beefy, very human guard who emerges and sounds a shattering "SHUSH!" every few minutes when the meter registers an unacceptable volume.

Speaking softly, Colalucci pointed toward the corner diagonally opposite and farthest away from us. At that time, the overhead lunette depicting two of Christ's ancestors, *Eleazar and Mathan*, by Michelangelo and, just below it, portraits of three of history's first thirty popes, by several other artists, were covered by a greenish opaque curtain behind which one could barely perceive six levels of scaffolding and an occasional human figure moving.

"That's as much as we'll cover at any one time during the restoration," Colalucci said, "because we want to keep the Sistine Chapel open to the public throughout." Having begun his mighty labor only in June 1980, and needing at least a couple of days a week to supervise other Vatican restorations, Colalucci concentrated on the lunette of *Eleazar and Mathan*, ancestors of Christ, according to St. Matthew, from the family of Ozias. Above them, on the edge of the ceiling itself, sits the prophet *Zachariah*, but the program called for *Eleazar and Mathan*'s restoration to be followed by work on the next lunette, *Jacob and Joseph*. Since the ceiling requires different techniques and equipment, *Zachariah*'s restoration must await that later phase.

Near the east exit wall, Colalucci unlocked a door under the curtain and admitted us to a small vestibule, where he told me to follow him up a series of three ladders—each two levels high, but one could hop off at the intermediate platform, too. Our first stop was the third platform, where we clambered off near the left shoulder of *Pope Marcellinus*, painted by Ghirlandaio.

"We do the least possible retouching when paint is missing," said Colalucci. "Do you see this large crack in the wall over this pope? It was touched up with paint in the eighteenth century, which created a problem: It won't look very nice when we've cleaned it. But the plan is to seal the crack so it doesn't crack again and then leave it looking this way."

Colalucci also called my attention to "a pope who has a hole in his head." He was *Pope Caius*, by Ghirlandaio's pupils, and his head wound was about the size of a grapefruit. It was badly filled in during an eighteenth-century restoration, and the filling almost fell out when the team started working around it. "So we'll put in a new piece, bring its surfaces together with proper adhesives and then touch it up because it's too large an area to leave open. But this is one of the few places where we're actually putting in paint."

On the topmost level, we stood some sixty feet in the air on a shaky plank at a height that was dizzying in every sense. Down below, the Sistine seemed less a chapel than a city square: a bustling Piazza del Popolo ebbing and flowing with people and noise, all punctuated by the insistent SHUSHing of the guard and the five-language tape recordings pleading in vain for silence.

One hundred and thirty feet, or half a city block, away, I could see *The Last Judgment* as I'd never seen it before: at distant eye level instead of at overpowering, overwhelming height. Up here, one becomes aware for the first time of the angels in the lunettes at the top, particularly the muscular angels bearing the Pillar of Flagellation, rather than of Charon and Minos and the damned.

Gazing upward, one sees near the center of the ceiling *The Creation of Adam*, seemingly the most damaged of the ceiling panels. Colalucci said he is not going to fill in the visible cracks. "In our restoration, we do the least possible. We'll solidify it, clean it and stop future damage. But we'll leave it as it is wherever we can."

Close to *Zachariah* in the center of the ceiling is the most damaged fresco of all. "Do you see those three nudes in *The Flood?*" Colalucci asked. "There used to be four. But, in 1797, there was an explosion of gunpowder in the Castel Sant' Angelo (more than a quarter of a mile away) and it created such a movement of air—like when a bullet leaves a gun—that the right-hand corner of the paint surface collapsed. Later, in a restoration toward the end of the nineteenth century, it was covered over with white paint and, since there's nothing of Michelangelo underneath, that's how we'll leave it."

In the ceiling spandrel nearest us—*Judith Covering the Head of Holofernes* (the head is thought by some to be a self-portrait of Michelangelo)—Colalucci pointed out "lots of brush strokes, badly done, during previous restorations. Actually, they weren't restorations so much as retouchings that painted substances into the ceiling which, then and there, made the frescoes look clean, but in time had the opposite effect and contributed to the pollution of the ceiling."

When Michelangelo finished the ceiling, a special curator, called a *mondatore*, was hired to keep the fresco clean by peeling off the dirty areas as they formed and hardened. "Today," Colalucci noted, "there's much more pollution in the air that penetrates the Sistine, which is a minus, but on the plus side we're now using substances which resist smog, unlike those in the past that formed chemical reactions with it. But if our work here is ever to be as meaningful as it ought to

be, something will have to be done to reduce the heat and humidity in the Sistine. The most damaging elements to frescoes are humidity and light. Light is less of a problem here since our windows don't admit much of it."

The restored figures of both *Eleazar and Mathan* looked gleaming and vivid, in startling contrast to their surroundings. "You can see three levels of restoration on Mathan," said Colalucci. "Beneath this horizontal line, it's cleaned and finished. From here up, it's had the first coating of dirt removed. And, above Mathan himself, it's very dark because it hasn't been cleaned yet."

Michelangelo painted Eleazar's leg in green and violet. "We've done nothing to this area except cleaning," said Colalucci, producing what looked like a pickle jar filled with slime. But the slime was a chemical solvent called AB57, or Pasta Mora, for it was developed by Professor and Mrs. Paolo Mora of Rome's Central Institute of Restoration, where Colalucci learned his art. "It was created mainly for marble, but the Moras experimented with it on frescoes. It's like a paste. It can be on for a minute or ten minutes. The effect varies with the amount of time it spends in contact with a surface. The danger is that if you leave it on a minute or two too long, it will go beyond the foreign substances and start removing the paint. So control of the time is crucial. You can see little areas where I've applied AB57 in two or three stages. Each time I take it off well before it's too late. Then I look at it and gauge how much more time it will need. Then I put it on again, but never too long."

Never? Sadly, Colalucci pointed to the purple part of Eleazar's leg. "Here's a tiny patch where I left it on too long. In this tiny little experimental patch, you see completely solid violet paint, but around it you can see

DELPHICA

ZACHERIAS

the gradations of darker and lighter, which are the shadings of Michelangelo's work."

What could be done now to restore the master's inch of subtlety to Eleazar's leg? "Nothing, because we seldom repaint, certainly never Michelangelo—not in the modern concept of restoration. In the old days, restorers used to prettify things by repainting, but after the Second World War the theory of restoration changed from making it pretty and filling in areas with the closest colors that made it look like it used to. Now we believe in the purity of the original work."

Down in the lower parts of the lunette, the Pasta Mora was applied for only three minutes, but the upper left-hand corner received applications lasting as long as three quarters of an hour. Why? "Because in olden times a leak of water formed a filmy calcium deposit up there. Now it takes the paste a good forty-five minutes to work through the calcium and dissolve it. You can still see the white stuff up there on the wall. That shiny cupid you're admiring was coated with calcium carbonate, and these figures were partly ruined by it. But repeated applications in small amounts of time saved the cupid."

We were distracted by a crunching noise two levels below. One of Colalucci's restorers was apparently carving up Ghirlandaio's fresco of *Pope Marcellinus*. "He's just applying clay before giving the pope an injection," explained Colalucci. "There's a crack along the pope and it's been cleaned. In about forty minutes, he'll inject a resin called Vinnapas—that's an acrylic vinylic, if you're interested—through a tiny hole he'll make in the center of the damaged area. And the clay he's using will enclose the area. Otherwise the resin would go right out instead of flowing in. Later, when the clay dries, it can be removed. It serves like the cork of a bottle to hold in fluid. We couldn't

Domenico Ghirlandaio, *Pope Marcellinus*, one of five surviving portraits of early popes painted by various artists. Others were painted over by Michelangelo.

158

just leave this crack, because just by touching the surface of the paint, we could tell it was detached. But this injection will reattach the paint substance to the wall." Later I learned from chief scientist Nazzareno Gabrielli that, in order to further minimize the danger of the resin's flowing out or away, the Vinnapas had been mixed with a solid substance: a fossil flour formed by crushing shells of plankton, or, as Gabrielli put it, "little organisms from the sea, refined into an inert substance that is not susceptible to humidity or any other kind of movement."

Turning back to the lunette, Colalucci continued: "Eleazar and Mathan were each painted in one day. All the lunettes were painted in the same technique: two main figures per lunette—one day for each main figure group plus one day for the center decoration.

"We know, from the actual level of the paint, that Michelangelo did the center first and then each of the figure groups. With the fresco technique, he couldn't afford any more time.

"Now the classical system of doing frescoes is to do sketches first, then the full-size cartoon, and then apply that to the wall, making the outline with a pointed ivory on the wet plaster surface.

"Instead, Michelangelo, *freehand*, did his drawing directly on the wall. We can tell you this because on this wall there are no dents, no dots, no incisions, no lines from pointed ivory—and in some places you can actually see Michelangelo's free design. In other places, he *did* use the cartoon method—but here, no."

Here is where drama develops daily before a restorer's eyes, for Colalucci is seeing the colors that were created by Michelangelo and the way he had to rush to make a change—a shoulder raised or lowered—before the plaster dried. Here is where Colalucci stands on the threshold of Michelangelo's mind.

In line with contemporary thinking, this restoration of the Sistine will concentrate on cleaning and solidifying, not retouching. To make a point, Colalucci gestured toward the darkish face peering at Mathan. "Is that her slave?" I asked.

"Same thing," he replied with a laugh. "It's her husband. The lady was very stingy and she was also the head of the house. Attached to her waist are the keys to her purse. The husband is looking at her with a worried, not very trusting expression. And she's bouncing the little cupid, who is, by the way, St. Joseph"—the earthly father of Jesus.

Colalucci continued: "Now, where the cupid is, it still appears very cracked, but it's actually quite solidified." Whereupon, with the confident hand of a professional, he rapped his fist on the lunette to prove his point.

"Art historians," he went on, "who have come and seen what little I've accomplished up here so far, say I'm making big problems for them because, as this restoration progresses, all of Michelangelo's work will have to be restudied. One of them said to me: 'Everything we've been saying about his colors and tones has been about the dirty Michelangelo, the sculptor and molder of three-dimensional form in painting. Now we will have to take a new look at Michelangelo the colorist. But now that you've dug out the dirt, we can see and almost touch the real Michelangelo. We will see the *pentimenti* where he changed his mind and had to act quickly before the plaster could dry. It will be a little like living again the moments of creation by Michelangelo—or like opening an Egyptian tomb. Or lifting a curtain and having this man Michelangelo step forward and say something about himself as a human being who could change his mind up here,

The original decoration of the Sistine Chapel consisted of scenes from the lives of Moses and Christ, painted by various artists. They were restored before work began on Michelangelo's frescoes in the chapel.

ABOVE Luca Signorelli, *Testament and Death of Moses*, 1482.

OPPOSITE ABOVE Domenico Ghirlandaio, *Christ Calling St. Peter and St. Andrew*, 1482.

OPPOSITE BELOW Perugino, *The Handing Over of the Keys to St. Peter*, 1481.

who could work impetuously, spontaneously, resourcefully, with improvisation, inspriation, dexterity and genius. Thank you for letting us live this discovery!' " Colalucci added a modest footnote: "Of course, all this depends upon the audience out front and has nothing to do with my work."

Time-consuming art historians themselves pose a problem for Colalucci and his crew of fresco restorers, so scholarly visits to the scaffold are confined to one day a week. But they are not the reason why the restoration of Michelangelo's frescoes will take Colalucci at least as long as it took Michelangelo to create them. Not only do his other duties limit his work, but even as the *Eleazar and Mathan* lunette reached completion, he would have to bide his time while his team completed the three popes, dismantled the scaffolding and, after the February 1981 unveiling, reassembled the platforms for moving on to the *Jacob and Joseph* lunette.

"By the time you're done," I asked, "will the Sistine be ready for another restoration?"

"No," Colalucci answered. "This one will last. It will be eternal. The greatest percentage of the damage has not been to the paintings; it's the substances put on *top* of the art over the centuries. So we are seeking to reduce to a minimum all these substances on the walls and ceiling. Without these extraneous chemical substances and with the science we have today, the frescoes will lead a long and happy and healthy life."

The next February, after the east wall had been unveiled, curator Mancinelli made an interesting observation: while there have been various restorations, the current one, to the best of his knowledge, is providing Michelangelo's work with only its third cleaning—its first in more than two and a half centuries. Aside from the periodic peelings of dirt by the *mondatore* of the Sistine Chapel, the first major cleaning was done around 1635 by a restorer named Lagi, who first dusted all the frescoes and then scrubbed them with bread crumbs wadded into balls. "Don't laugh!" said Mancinelli. "It was probably a very good cleaner, since the frescoes weren't so dirty as they get now. The dirt was mostly powder then and the bread crumbs worked like an eraser. Later, as dirt became dirtier and more chemical, such simple solutions no longer worked, but the real trouble started in the nineteenth century, when restorers began using resins and glues to make the frescoes more brilliant. Oh, they seemed very effective then, but they create problems now."

The second cleaning came early in the eighteenth century and was done by Carlo Maratta (1625–1713), the Baroque painter whose brilliant 1669 portrait of Pope Clement IX hangs in the Pinacoteca and who also restored various frescoes in the Raphael Rooms. While it has long been known that Eleazar's left foot—which points downward dramatically to parallel a left arm whose vivid eloquence reminds some of the arms in *The Creation* ceiling panels—was not by Michelangelo, it can now be surmised that the original foot, which must have been totally damaged, was made anew by Maratta. "The quality of that foot," said Mancinelli, "is higher than any other remaking we've encountered in the Sistine Chapel. It was beautifully made by a good painter. Maratta was the only artist of such caliber who ever worked up there after Michelangelo's time, so he must be the one. It couldn't possibly have been done very long after Maratta's time because this foot has the same tone as the rest of the fresco while all other additions were out of tone with Michelangelo, meaning that the fresco was dirty and the retouchers simply imitated the dirty colors they could see. Right after Maratta's cleaning, it was

One of the damned, in *The Last Judgment*, dragged down to Hell.

Michelangelo, *The Prophet Joel*.

still possible to perceive Michelangelo's tones, but not for too much longer—and then not until now."

While the restorations of the nineteenth century, with their glues and resins, may have done as much harm as good, they had one element in common with the twentieth-century restoration that Mancinelli considers "a perfect work." It was done from 1923 to 1945. "None of them did any real cleaning. Oh, there may have been a superficial cleaning, but we have no record of anything major and, if there had been one, we would not have found the frescoes as dirty as we've found them." But that one "perfect" job, initiated under Director-General Bartolomeo Nogara, was a rescue operation that concentrated on consolidating the ceiling and

fixing plaster to walls, without which Colalucci and his cohorts might not have had so much to work with today.

Another discovery of the current restoration has been that, except for the restored left foot, the entire *Eleazar and Mathan* lunette was completed by Michelangelo. In several other lunettes, there are parts that can be attributed to assistants. The main figures were always by Michelangelo, but sometimes he left parts to his helpers. For example, every lunette has an identifying panel between its two parts and, above the frame of each inscription, what Mancinelli calls "an architectonic head formed as a mask. Now we can see that the mask over the names of Eleazar and Mathan is surely by Michelangelo, just as I can

Three scenes from the ceiling: ABOVE *God Creates the Sun and the Moon*. OPPOSITE ABOVE *The Drunkenness of Noah*. OPPOSITE BELOW *The Flood*. One of the figures framing this scene was destroyed when a gunpowder explosion in the Castel Sant' Angelo created vibrations that caused the painted surface to collapse. The gap was covered with white paint in the nineteenth century, which Colalucci will leave as it is.

already tell you that the one over the names of Jacob and Joseph is not. Its style is more feeble, less certain—clearly not the same vigorous hand that did the rest of the lunette."

Noting that "this is the first time in our lives that we can see the real colors of Michelangelo," Mancinelli went on to say that "now we can understand why he was so important to the Mannerists," those sixteenth-century artists like Muziano and, to a certain extent, Cellini, who rebelled against the High Renaissance's equilibrium of form and proportions with such weapons as distortion, harsh lighting and colors that can be described as intense, often strident, sometimes even violent. "The very peculiar range of colors that we're starting to see with this cleaning," said Mancinelli, "are the colors that were later imitated by Mannerist painters." As an example, he cited the combination of greens and violets on Eleazar's right leg, "the use of pure tones and acid colors, a little bit bitter and somewhat coarse." Some of Michelangelo's greens, he added, were applied in *secco*—on dry plaster—and had virtually vanished; what had been done in true fresco—on wet plaster—was in nearly perfect condition.

The *pentimenti*—those changes of Michelangelo's mind which emerged before Colalucci's and Mancinelli's eyes during the cleaning of the lunette—tell the most about the way the man worked. "With the head of Mathan," said the curator, "you can perceive his exceptional quickness. First, he draws a rough silhouette, just to have an idea of the position of the head on the wall. Then he looks for the contour three or four times. Later in the day, he changes his contours a little. He lowers Mathan's mantle and moves the headband below it to a different position. You can see the pink coloration under the mantle in the part where the band used to be.

Up close, you can also see how he lowered Eleazar's shoulder. You're so near that it's like watching Michelangelo work.

"What you see is how instinctive and emotional he was—just plunging right ahead with astonishing certainty. One of the things we learn from the *pentimenti* is the remarkable fact that there are just so few *pentimenti*. It's crazy that anybody could work so fast, let alone so well. He must have been born just to create.

"In his sculpture as well as his painting, you sense some of the violence and immediacy of the way he worked. He sculpted as he painted—by starting with the dark parts. With a fresco, first he molds the figure on the wall. When he carves, he takes off the figure from the stone. Later, he moves from dark to light: first the shades, then the lighted parts.

"Many of these ideas about him were fairly firmly theorized. But now, with the cleaning of the Sistine Chapel, they are becoming very, very evident."

The Sistine Chapel was unscaffolded for only two weeks before work continued on the rest of the east wall: Michelangelo's lunette of *Jacob and Joseph*. It was estimated that this and the dozen remaining Michelangelo lunettes of Christ's ancestors, plus the remaining twenty-one papal portraits (four of the original thirty were obliterated by Michelangelo when he painted *The Last Judgment* on the west wall) and the rest of the *trompe l'oeil* curtain would take a good four years. The ceiling will require four more years, as well as the construction of a scaffold with a movable platform that will ride on rails, can be raised and lowered, won't obscure too much of the public's view and will have a flexible reclining back support so that Colalucci will not have to restore the ceiling on his back the way Charlton Heston did in the movie. It is myth that Michelangelo did it that way. "It would have been physically impossible," says Mancinelli. "The distance was too great. But we also have a book of Michelangelo's poems which has a sketch by him of how he worked on the Sistine ceiling—and he is standing." Colalucci's platform will be modeled in part on Michelangelo's sketch.

Only when the ceiling is completed will the entire *Last Judgment* on the west wall disappear from view for an estimated four years. Mancinelli explained why the west wall must be done "together and totally" rather than piecemeal: "We shall start cleaning it the way Michelangelo painted it: from top to bottom. But, to get to the top, you have to start building your scaffolding from the bottom. And you have to clean a whole work before you can begin retouching. Besides, to retouch, you have to take into account the whole surface, the balance of parts.

"Yes, there will be retouching because there are parts where color has been lost and parts that were repainted later, not just in Michelangelo's time. Some small nineteenth-century additions will be removed *if* we find the original Michelangelo underneath, which I hope we will, though I imagine they were painted over because they were damaged. Where we cannot restore or retouch the original Michelangelo, we will probably leave what is there."

Technically, *The Last Judgment* will be the most difficult phase of the Sistine restoration, for, to a greater extent than any other work of Michelangelo's in the chapel, it was painted in *secco* (on dry plaster) with pigments having a glue or casein base. This poses more problems than true fresco, the technique of painting on a moist lime plaster surface with colors ground in water or a limewater mixture; the lime provides a binder, which, in drying, forms a calcium carbonate that blends pigment with wall.

"All our time estimates are very vague," Mancinelli admitted, "because we will proceed with caution and because, in restoration, you really never know what *all* your problems will be until you are faced with them. And, before we even touch *The Last Judgment*, we want to have the experience of the lunettes and the ceiling behind us. Because, looking ahead, we know that the ultimate judgment of the whole restoration will be made by millions and millions of people who will come to look at that wall for what will truly be the first time."

TAPESTRY
RESTORATION
LABORATORY

FROM FERRAZZA'S OFFICE IN the oldest part of the Papal Palace, we descend to the Courtyard of the Pappagallo, so named for a noisy parrot that used to be kept in a room upstairs, and make our way down a ramp through the Belvedere Court, nowadays perhaps the world's only parking lot built by Bramante, and into the heart of Vatican City. Past the main post office, on a side street to the left—next door to the offices of *L'Osservatore Romano*, the daily newspaper of the Holy See—stands a red-tiled building whose door is opened only when you ring thrice in a prearranged musical rhythm. Inside, you step into a scene of serenity, diligence and devotion. It is a cloistered workshop that few visitors to the Vatican ever see.

At one end of a large airy high-ceilinged room whose six overhead windows usually admit more than enough light to work by, three white-robed nuns of a French order, the Missionaries of Mary, are just beginning to put together a precious, tattered tapestry that looks as if a dog has chewed it beyond

recognition. Above them hangs a magnificent turn-of-the-nineteenth-century tapestry reproduction of Caravaggio's *Descent from the Cross*, the original of which now hangs in the Pinacoteca up the hill. The painting was one of the first Vatican treasures removed by Napoleon in 1797, and during its nearly two-decade stay in Paris, this copy was made.

"I love Caravaggio," says Soeur Sebastia, the tiny seventy-eight-year-old nun who heads the Tapestry Restoration Laboratory. "I think he's a great artist. But I think the man who made this tapestry is an even greater artist."

At the other end of the workshop, three women who are not nuns are sewing finishing touches onto parts of a Gobelin they have restored. This laboratory was founded in 1926, but the only reminders of the twentieth century are the portable radios used by two of the secular weavers.

There is much that is modern, however,

OPPOSITE Soeur Sebastia, center, head of the Tapestry Restoration Laboratory, at work with members of her staff. The racks behind them hold six thousand different colors of thread, all hand-dyed in the laboratory.

about this old-fashioned workshop. Soeur Sebastia opens some cabinets against one wall to show me that there are no fewer than six thousand different colors of thread on her racks. "We dye them ourselves," she says. "They all come to us white. For my first quarter of a century here, we dyed our threads with vegetable oils, but they all had the danger that sun could fade them and washing could spoil them. Then, in the 1960s, the chemists told us about a dye from Ciba that was all chemical with none of these risks. We tried it and it worked." But each time they changed dyes, Soeur Sebastia would wrap a sample of thread she'd dyed dark blue around a card and leave it out on her terrace in the Vatican for a month to make sure that the color would be unchanged by the elements.

"I chose dark blue," she explains, "because dark blue and dark brown are the two most delicate colors and dark blue is the more sensitive of the two; it fades fastest and is more susceptible to the elements. Dark brown is the color of silk and that's what usually is destroyed first in a tapestry. But now we are no longer using silk thread because the factories have found a kind of synthetic cotton that is more resistant."

"But doesn't it show on a restoration?" I ask.

"No," she replies. "Silk is always shiny, but the new silk is always shinier than the old silk. When we use this thread, however, with two or three other threads blended into it, the result is shiny—don't ask me why—but it can be matched to the shade of the old silk."

Mostly, though, Soeur Sebastia sticks to time-honored methods and materials that she trusts. Every tapestry brought in for restoration is first given a ritual bath in an immense tub: immersion in cold water overnight followed by washing with an ancient root she calls *radica saponaria*, or soap root. The sisters boil the root until it forms a foam, into which they dip brushes and scrub the tapestry with the suds. "It is miraculous," she marvels, "how just this much care brings back the color." But the Vatican's supply of soap root is down to a couple of years at most, for while it used to be available at almost any Roman art-supply store, it recently disappeared from the market. Soeur Sebastia suspects the chemical companies have bought it up as a base for their commercial detergents, some of which have been tested by the Vatican Museums scientific laboratories and pronounced satisfactory. "But," she says, "until we run out of soap root, we will stay with what has worked for centuries."

At the other end of the workshop from "our threads" are "our wools," neatly classified by color in some three hundred numbered plastic packages. Within each of these packages, however, are some twenty to twenty-five gradations of the color. Once a year, the six women sift through these packets to see what is missing or used up and then they dye the replacements. This inventory process takes them three full weeks.

How does Soeur Sebastia match a color of thread or wool with that of the tapestry being restored? "Of course, we compare it with the original material on the tapestry," she replies, "after we've made the selection from our cupboard. But this only confirms that we've picked the right one the first time just by looking.

"You need an artist's passion to do this," she continues. "And you can only do a little at a time. Three people can take two or three years just to repair one tapestry. Those three girls [as she calls the women who work for her] started with us when they were students at the Academy of Fine Arts in Rome and have been with us for fifteen years or more.

Raphael, *The Miraculous Draught of Fishes*, 1515–16, tapestry woven in the workshop of Pieter van Aelst, Brussels.

School of Raphael, *Massacre of the Innocents*, 1520s, tapestries woven in the workshop of Pieter van Aelst, Brussels.

We all work in perfect harmony. My two sisters here are Spanish. They had some experience in an embroidery workshop in Spain. My story is a little different."

She is Hungarian, and when she joined the order she wanted to be a missionary in China. But she did her novitiate in the Vatican and when a woman who worked in the relatively new tapestry lab took sick, the Hungarian novice was sent down there to fill in for a fortnight. "Those two weeks seemed like an eternity," she recalls, "but they have turned into only a lifetime."

The woman she replaced never returned to work, and Pope Pius XI decreed that Soeur Sebastia would stay—as she has since 1933. When she pleaded that she longed to be a missionary, the Pope told her: "Your mission is right here, not in China."

She was, and is, obedient, philosophical. "In the beginning," she says, "patience is the hardest part. . . . I used to paint when I was a girl. In painting, you see the results very soon, often immediately. Here, it can be years before you see the result."

A tapestry restoration can take months or years. "When you start," says Soeur Sebastia, "you never know when you will finish." Her workshop can never hope to handle more than four major orders per year. Since 1976, her entire force has been coping with a series of six sixteenth-century Flemish tapestries retelling the Greek myth of Cephalus and Procris, the saga of twisted and tragically tested marital fidelity whose beginning we glimpsed on a bronze mirror in the Etruscan Museum, when we saw the dawn goddess Eos (Aurora), enamored of the hunter Cephalus, abducting him to Syria. Repulsed by Cephalus's fidelity to his wife, Procris, Eos sent Cephalus home in disguise to test his spouse's constancy. Resisting the handsome stranger at first, Procris finally gave in to his blandishments and rich gifts.

Enraged, Cephalus revealed his true identity and drove her from his house. Banished, Procris was befriended by Apollo's twin sister, Artemis, who gave her further gifts, including a javelin that never missed its mark and a hunting dog that always caught its quarry. Then Procris returned to Cephalus and won him back with *her* gifts. Under such circumstances, it is not surprising that now *she* was tormented by doubts of *his* fidelity, so she followed him secretly on one of his hunts. Hearing something stirring in the foliage, Cephalus hurled his infallible javelin at the sound. Upon discovering that he had mortally wounded his wife, Cephalus hurled himself from a cliff into the sea.

With three or four women working on one job (with only incidental months out for Gobelins or other "rush" jobs), they've taken six months to do one of the series, two years to do another and intermediate times to do three more. They started the final one in August 1980 and when last visited had no idea when they would finish.

For a year before World War II and much of a decade after, the three sisters collaborated with six or seven other women on their most notable achievement: restoring two different tapestry copies of Leonardo da Vinci's *The Last Supper*.

Though Soeur Sebastia cherishes the genius of Leonardo, she, as a restorer, reserves her ultimate professional admiration for tapestry-makers, whether they are weaving originals or copies. "The reason is simple," she says. "Restoration is done from the front. But originals are done from behind with mirrors to enable the weaver to see what he is doing. Of course, some of *our* work has to be done with mirrors, too, from behind."

Restoring the first Leonardo copy, a

OPPOSITE School of Raphael, *The Supper at Emmaus*, 1520s, tapestry woven in the workshop of Pieter van Aelst, Brussels.

sixteenth-century Flemish tapestry, was backbreaking labor, for it was thirty feet long and sixteen feet high and in such bad shape that it could not be folded or rolled the way all other tapestries are during restoration. Carpenters built a long table in a special hall of the building to accommodate the tapestry and its ten restorers, who had to work standing up and bending over it from above, rather than seated near eye and hand level.

The first problem with this copy was that it had several holes. A cloth was placed beneath each hole, and new and stronger woolen threads matching the surviving old threads were sewn into the supporting cloth until everything adhered and was reinforced by the cloth.

The second problem was that the silk tablecloth of *The Last Supper* was so completely ruined that it had to be replaced with a new silk cloth, which the sisters wove. On such occasions, even a restoration is done from behind with mirrors as with originals. "Silk is always a problem," says Soeur Sebastia. "It is so delicate that it ruins fastest."

Finally, on all of the disciples' heads except one, "the wool was in terrible condition" and had to be rewoven. The exception was Judas Iscariot. Soeur Sebastia pronounces this "interesting," but refuses to reflect aloud on the durability of evil. More relevant today is that with Leonardo's fading fresco off display in Milan and its future in limbo, this copy—lately hung like a theatre curtain in the fourth room of the Pinacoteca —is perhaps the most impressive *Last Supper* presently on public view in Italy.

The second Leonardo copy was a more silken *Last Supper*, made in the tapestry workshop of San Michele in nearby Trastevere and copied not from the fresco but from the Vatican's Flemish tapestry around 1780. This was a period when tapestry-makers experimented with weaving vertically in silk and horizontally in silk and wool. Silk is so delicate that hardly any of these works survived, and after a few decades weavers went back to letting wool predominate. In the twentieth century, the sisters and their co-workers found the vertical silk threads not merely ruined but pulverized. So they replaced them, silk strand by silk strand, with thin cotton threads: virtually a labor of creation, again involving working from behind with mirrors. To make matters worse, as they worked on the horizontal silk threads, the wool threads would break, raise up or shift, so they had to restore or replace the wool, too. And the borders were in such terrible condition that they had to be restored with cloth backing. Some silk remains, but this second *Last Supper* tapestry is now mostly cotton.

The final result of this postwar restoration, finished in 1954, was hung behing Pope Pius XII when he used to celebrate Mass outdoors in St. Peter's Square. When I asked Soeur Sebastia what pride she felt then, she replied: "The tapestry didn't interest me at such times. All I cared about was to take part in the Mass and all I regret is that Masses are no longer held outside." Since Pius XII, however, four popes have brought out this *Last Supper* tapestry for ceremonial occasions in the Papal Apartments.

Not long ago, one of them, John Paul II, visited this cloister of craftwomanship that few men have ever invaded. After a few minutes there, a member of the Holy Father's entourage called his attention, on the back of a tapestry, to the traces of a gaping hole that the women had obliterated perfectly from front view.

"Can you see what they have managed to do?" the aide marveled.

"I do not see," the Pope replied. "I only admire."

Tapestries woven in Tournai in the fifteenth century are among those displayed in the richly decorated Gallery of Tapestries, installed in 1838 during the reign of Pope Gregory XVI.

RESTORING THE PIETA

A T 11:30 ON THE MORNING of Whitsunday, May 21, 1972, when the Pontifical Mass for Pentecost had ended in St. Peter's Basilica and worshippers were making their way out to the square, a young Hungarian-born Australian named Laszlo Toth leaped into the side chapel housing Michelangelo's marble *Pietà*, pulled out a hammer hidden under his coat and dealt the incomparable Madonna fifteen blows that smashed her left eye and part of her nose, broke her left arm into three fragments, knocked off all five of her left fingers, chipped her cheek and her mantle and dented the back of her head. The Christ figure was undamaged, for the assailant, who was quickly captured, later told interrogators that he considered himself the son of God, but did not recognize this woman as his mother.

Though more than fifty fragments of the *Pietà* were swiftly scooped up by guards, the mutilation at first looked hopeless to the experts who converged upon the scene that Sunday afternoon. The broken pieces were taken up the hill to the Vatican Museums restoration laboratories. Although the art treasures in St. Peter's are not in the Museums' collection, it was agreed that the Museums' laboratories, then presided over by Dr. Vittorio Federici and his assistant, Nazzareno Gabrielli, offered the best restoration facilities.

The two scientists quickly established that only a few tiny shards of marble seemed to be missing, probably lost or totally pulverized in the scuffle that followed the attack. And there was one other crucial blessing: more than twenty years earlier, a modeler named Luigi Mercatali had made a perfect plaster cast of the *Pietà* under Vatican auspices for conservation in the treasury of St. Peter's. When the *Pietà* went to the New York World's Fair in 1964, this copy had been displayed in St. Peter's during its absence.

Dr. Deoclecio Redig de Campos, then the director-general of the Vatican Museums,

OPPOSITE Michelangelo's *Pietà*, 1499–1500, is displayed in a side chapel of St. Peter's.

Ulderico Grispigni, the Vatican Museums' chief sculpture restorer.

concluded that any part of the *Pietà* that was
missing or hopelessly mutilated could be
exactly duplicated in undamaged form from
Mercatali's direct impression of the original.
That fact, more than any other, dictated the
decision to attempt to restore the figure to its
pristine condition. As de Campos, now
retired, explains: "The extraordinary
perfection of the *Pietà* is one of its essential
characteristics. It would not have tolerated
gaps or completion in a material other than
marble from Carrara."

When de Campos relayed his findings to
the highest level of the Vatican, his decision
was accepted, but the choice of restorers
required several months of weighty
discussion and intense debate both inside
and outside the Vatican: whether to use the
Vatican Museums' restorers and technicians,
call in Italian experts or import others from
abroad and overseas. The sculptor Manzù
was briefly mentioned as a candidate to head
the team. Finally it was decided to do the job
"in house" for several reasons, one of them
being that the Vatican Museums' chief
marble restorer, Ulderico Grispigni, had
learned his art under *Pietà* modeler
Mercatali, who used to work as an outside
contractor carrying out restorations and
making copies for various Vatican and
Roman museums. Grispigni proudly
proclaims himself an *"autodidatta"*—
meaning, in his case, a self-taught school
dropout (at fourteen). He worked his way into
Mercatali's workshop and was employed
there from 1953 until 1966, when the aging
Mercatali (who died a few years later)
recommended him to Vatican Museums
officials with these words: "Take Grispigni.
He will do honor to you." At the time, the
only personnel slot open was a probationary
appointment as a maintenance man, but
Grispigni took it just to be on the payroll
when an impending vacancy materialized.

Seven months later he left the maintenance department to become a sculpture restorer.

The seven-man team that de Campos put together included himself; Grispigni; scientists Gabrielli and Federici; Francesco Dati, a master restorer of bronzes and paintings who was chosen for his insights into colors and resins; plasticist Giuseppe Morresi, a modest restorer who makes everything from masks and molds of masterpieces to identification badges; and Francesco Vacchini, the engineer in charge of St. Peter's. The work begun in the labs before the team was chosen had already produced complete photographic and plastic documentation of the damage. Now every single detail of the planned restoration would be tried out first on blocks of marble identical to the marble of the *Pietà*. All other materials to be used would be tested with an electronic dynamometer to measure their adhesiveness and resistance under pressure. Inferior and damaged statues not worth saving would have their arms broken and reattached, new eyes and fingers implanted, to test techniques. Chemists worked overtime finding formulas to dissolve every possible kind of grease film that might be formed by the solvents that would be used. Any step that wasn't completely successful in these trials was dropped or subjected to further research, for the technicians had to anticipate that whatever could go wrong in the lab might well go wrong on the *Pietà*.

Behind the wooden fence that shielded the *Pietà*'s chapel from public view, Gabrielli built a mini-laboratory in the recesses and Grispigni started building a platform that would enable him to work at the right level. One Saturday that summer, de Campos asked Grispigni about his progress and then told him: "Fine! On Monday, you start working with the *Pietà*." Grispigni hardly slept the next two nights.

On Monday morning, he went up to the main lab to sort the fragments into two categories: body and clothing. But there was a third category: small pieces that couldn't yet be classified.

Intimidating though all these fragments of various sizes were, sorting them into trays and then scraping each piece clean with a pointer reminiscent of a dentist's implement gave Grispigni confidence as he felt for himself how much had been saved.

A couple of days later, however, when he moved down to St. Peter's, his jitters returned. "The thing that made all of us nervous," he recalled, "was having all those eyes upon us." He meant that, even behind a wooden fence, "if our work hadn't been satisfactory, everybody in the world would have seen. . . . Besides, there were always cardinals dropping in to see how we were doing."

Grispigni plunged into the work he does best, starting with the Virgin's face, so disfigured that he found it hard to confront. Grispigni, a forty-five-year-old Roman, has an almost personal relationship with the Virgin Mary. When he speaks of the *Pietà* today, he says the Madonna had the patience of someone waiting in a dentist's chair to be drilled and torn, pummeled and pasted, but eventually healed.

The restoration team began with the nose, broken off at the tip into three pieces that had all been recovered. The only missing piece was one that didn't show: a tiny sliver on the inside of the left nostril. But, working from his silicone rubber impression of the Mercatali cast, plasticist Morresi was able to duplicate the missing sliver, and after all four pieces had been glued together with a polyester resin, this solid piece was reattached to the nose by Grispigni with de Campos and Federici giving directions. Twenty hours were needed for the resin to

The profile of the Madonna, before and after restoration. Says restorer
Grispigni, "We gave this beautiful lady her face back."

solidify into a modern mastic even harder than marble. Overnight, the nose was propped up by little cotton-tipped strips of wood extending upward from the body of Christ as their base.

"The whole process was reversible," Grispigni observes. If anything had gone wrong, the mastic, which is soluble in acetone, could have been removed and the team would have started over. "As it was, when I pushed the nose on, a little bit of mastic oozed out and had to be cleaned off before it hardened. But someone was standing by with a special solvent that was applied with cotton and got rid of it right away."

The next day, without prearrangement, every member of the team reported to work in St. Peter's at least an hour or two early. "And when we saw and touched and felt that the mastic not only held one hundred percent, but that there was no discoloration, no water, no bubble of anything," Grispigni says, "then we began to relax."

Next came the much more delicate eye repair. Two of the eye injuries were, in de Campos's words, "of very small dimensions but vital esthetic importance because they deformed the Virgin's face unbearably." Two tiny fragments were missing from the lid of the left eye: one from the area nearest the tear duct and the other from the central part of the eyelid. Even if Morresi could duplicate the missing fragments, working from his rubber impression of the Mercatali cast, the *Pietà*'s left eye would still have a glassy, unseeing, false look. But then, in the middle of yet another sleepless night, Grispigni remembered a small fragment of marble sitting in his "unclassified" tray in the laboratory:

"I'd had this beautiful fragment in my hand so many times, but I couldn't place it. I didn't know where it went. It was curved,

modeled, clearly an outside surface. I'd put it in different places trying to find the one and only place it should go. I'm sure I'd tried the eye earlier, but I must have made some mistake. Now, in the middle of the night, I was sure that's where it went. I lay twitching in bed until dawn and was at the lab just as soon as I could get in and sign the piece out. It was hardly as big as the nail of my little finger. I took it down to St. Peter's. As I walked toward the statue, I knew. It seemed as if she knew, too, and was just waiting. I tried it in the eye and it fit."

It was the crucial fragment of the eyelid near the tear duct and, once it was reattached, it was far easier for Morresi to reconstruct the missing central part of the eyelid. Easier, but not easy. He had to make ten tries at the eye prosthesis before he could eliminate a minute discrepancy bit by bit. When the reconstructed fragment fit perfectly, Morresi studied it under a microscope to ascertain that his gradations of marble crystals and color were correct before attaching the piece to the eye. He used long cotton swab sticks to hold it in place for twenty hours.

"The greatest moment of joy for me," Grispigni says, "had been when I'd stuck that piece back in the eye and realized it had come from there. That night, I slept perfectly and dreamed that the *Pietà* would come out beautifully in the end. And I didn't have a bad night's sleep from then on."

They did the mantle next. Thirteen fragments first had to be joined together perfectly, for only if this solid mass were the right size could it be properly reattached near the Virgin's face. It was.

The greatest technical problems of all attended the next phase: restoration of the Madonna's left arm. The maniac's hammer, pounding from above and behind, had broken off the arm at the shoulder and severed it at the elbow as well. To make matters worse, when the forearm fell, it broke at the wrist and immediately the fingers came off, too. The fingers were the least of anybody's worries, for they were not by Michelangelo, but part of an eighteenth-century restoration. They were reattached in perfect position in a matter of minutes, working from a rubber impression Morresi had made of the Mercatali cast. The big problem was to put the three sections—upper arm, forearm and hand—back together to recreate an arm, bent outward, which had been carved exquisitely out of a single block of marble.

The answer, now a textbook example in restoration classes around the world, was a feat of orthopedic surgery. A stainless steel pin was fashioned to bend at the elbow, at just the right angle when inserted through the three parts of the arm. An L-shaped drill was used to bore holes exactly twelve millimeters (less than half an inch) in diameter—one millimeter (.04 inch) wider than the pin—into all three fragments only after painstaking experimentation with the angle and hole sites on impressions made by Morresi. The drill would travel forward only six centimeters (2.36 inches) at a time, so that Grispigni could constantly check to be sure that the path being cut was centered.

The steel pin, made to order in the Vatican's mechanical workshop, had narrow grooves along two of its sides. Once the fragmented limb had been joined provisionally by the pin, plastic tubes were inserted in the pin's grooves and, by means of a suction pump, a gluing resin was sucked through the tubes into the hollowed-out cavity. A smaller, easily detachable tube was attached to the main tubes' exit point and, when gluing resin began to appear in this smaller tube, the team could guess that the cavity was filled with the fluid that would bind pin and dismembered arm into one secure whole. Both tubes were then sealed by Morresi with Wacker RTV silicone gum for the obligatory twenty hours, and the next day, the detachable tube was removed and the others were cut and tied like an umbilical cord.

"I'd had no better idea than to drill a hole through the statue's shoulder and send the resin down from there," Grispigni says. "But that would have meant damaging an undamaged part, which might not have shown, but wouldn't have been right. It took a chemist like Gabrielli to suggest sucking the resin upward through the tube. Once he broached the idea, I knew he was on the right track even before his lab trials showed it could be done."

Viewed up close, which is scarcely possible nowadays with the *Pietà* behind unbreakable bulletproof glass, the only discernible casualties of the 1972 attack are the Madonna's fingers, which look as though they have rings or extra knuckles where they were reattached. This is deliberate, as are the four hammer dents that have been left in the back of her skull as a record of the 1972 restoration that will be remembered as part of the *Pietà*'s history.

When all of the *Pietà*'s parts had been reattached and restored (the piece of eyelid, the inner nostril sliver and some fragments of the robe were the only significant missing segments that had to be re-created by Morresi), another problem remained. On some sections of the statue that had withstood the attack were blue spots from the assailant's hammer. They were traces of a dye applied by the manufacturer to keep the hammer from rusting. Trying to remove these stains with cleaning fluid might have harmed the marble or left little circles around the spots the way spot-removers do on

The *Pietà*, before and after restoration. The difficult repair of the Madonna's
left arm was accomplished so skillfully that the breaks are completely invisible.

clothes. But Dati, the bronze restorer (who died in 1980), suggested a solution that didn't involve solvents: applying Scotch tape to the blue spots for a few minutes and then ripping the tape off. It worked.

The final phase was to dust the whole statue. Then Grispigni, Morresi and Dati washed it little by little with sponges soaked in cold distilled water. As they worked, they could see the ravaged but rebuilt *Pietà* regain its gleaming luster.

The restoration was completed four days before Christmas 1972, exactly seven months to the day of the disaster. And, on a Sunday in early 1973, Pope Paul VI reconsecrated the *Pietà*'s chapel with a sermon from his window in the Apostolic Palace and then announced that he was coming down to bless the statue (via his special elevator from the Pauline Chapel to St. Peter's). The crowd in St. Peter's Square rushed into the basilica to see both the *Pietà* and the pope. Standing behind the glass draperies in the statue's chapel, "Lillo" Grispigni, wearing his best blue suit instead of the usual white smock, knew that his privileged intimacy with the Madonna was at an end.

On a warm Wednesday in October 1980, while Pope John Paul II was making a public appearance in St. Peter's Square and the basilica behind him was closed, Grispigni, Morresi and a security guard named Adriano Rosati took me behind the bulletproof glass to show me their *Pietà*: the first of four that Michelangelo started, but the only one he completed—and, in fact, the only work he ever signed. Overhearing two visitors from Lombardy attributing it one day to a mediocre artist from their hometown, Michelangelo went back that night into the church with his chisel to carve into the ribbon across the Virgin's breast: "MICHAEL. ÄGELUS. BONAROTUS. FLORENT. FACIEBAT."

(MICHELANGELO BUONARROTI, FLORENTINE, MADE IT.)

Morresi pointed out that the lines in the palm of the Madonna's left hand form an "M." Rosati suggested that Michelangelo was putting his initial there, but Grispigni held up his own hand, surprisingly uncalloused for an artisan's, and said: "Look, everybody has an M pattern in the palm of his hand. It's just that some are stronger than others."

"Yes," said Morresi, "but who else but Michelangelo knew so much about the human body to put it in?"

Plasticist Morresi pointed out another fascinating detail. "Look closely at the little area between the left breast of Christ and the right breast of the Madonna," he instructed. "In the creases of her gown, you can perceive a death's head in the folds. Now look at the right side of the ribbon she's wearing. Do you see the face of a child in the marble?" Morresi believes Michelangelo put or left these patterns in the marble to symbolize life and death. He and Grispigni added that both the Virgin and Christ had at one time been given haloes by an early restorer.

None of these details, not even Michelangelo's signature, is visible through the bulletproof glass, but Grispigni accepted the inevitability of precautions after the madman's attack had pointed up the vulnerability of the *Pietà*.

"Just being here," Grispigni remarked almost a decade after the restoration, "brings back so many memories of those months: the tension, the happiness. Every piece we put back was a moment in history for me that I'll always remember."

"We would meet here at eight every morning," said Morresi, "and exchange ideas about how we were going to handle the day's tasks. No matter how much we'd planned and practiced, we always had new thoughts that had come to us in the night."

"I kept telling myself on the way in," said Grispigni, "that if you go at the job with too much emotion, with trembling and timidity, then you won't be able to do it right. But I could be a little more secure just because every single thing I did down here had been rehearsed many times."

Grispigni took a last look at the *Pietà* as we were leaving. "If you ask any of us twenty years from now what we did with our lives," he said, "I think we will tell you the same answer you'd get now: 'We gave this beautiful lady her face back.'"

Altar Cross commissioned by Cardinal Alessandro Farnese for the main altar of St. Peter's, 1582, silver-gilt with rock crystal intaglio plaques; silver by Antonio Gentili da Faenza; plaques by Valerio Belli.

ACKNOWLEDGMENTS

The author wishes to thank, in addition to the persons cited in his text, Patricia Bonicatti, Guido Colelli, Linda Graham, Maurizio Sabatucci and Luigi Venditti of the Vatican Museums; Judy Allen, Dr. Franca Camiz, Jeff and Linda Davidson, Milton Gendel and Minister Plenipotentiary Rodolfo Siviero of Rome; Erika, Monica and Valerie Levy, Dr. Hermann Prossinger and Irene Rooney of Vienna; Milton Esterow, Sylvia Hochfield, John L. Hochmann, Amy Newman, Janet Wilson, Alexandria Hatcher, Wendy Moonan, Herbert Rosenberg and John and Margaret Williamson of New York. This book was written on a Lanier AES Plus word processor through the courtesy of Robert Tonko, Vienna.

A.L.

PHOTO CREDITS

Candlesticks commissioned by Cardinal Alessandro Farnese for the main altar of St. Peter's, 1582, silver-gilt with rock crystal intaglio plaques; silver by Antonio Gentili da Faenza; plaques by Valerio Belli.

An Artpress Book

Chairman: Milton Esterow
President and Editor-in-Chief: John L. Hochmann
Managing Editor: Ray F. Patient
Senior Editor: Sylvia Hochfield
Copy Editor: Katherine Ness
Proofreader: Miriam Hurewitz
Editorial Assistant: Nancy Schwartz
Designer: Joseph Bourke Del Valle
Cover Design: Nora Sheehan
Floor Plan Artist: Mike Madrid
Art Assistants: Barbara Bedick, Dolores R. Santoliquido